THE COMPLETE GUIDE TO WRITING EFFECTIVE & AWARD-WINNING GRANTS

Step-by-Step Instructions

By Dianne Harris

THE COMPLETE GUIDE TO WRITING EFFECTIVE & AWARD-WINNING GRANTS — **STEP-BY-STEP INSTRUCTIONS**

1405 SW 6th Ave. • Ocala, Florida 34471 • 800-814-1132 • 352-622-1875—Fax
Web site: www.atlantic-pub.com • E-mail: sales@atlantic-pub.com
SAN Number: 268-1250

ISBN-13: 978-1-60138-046-3 ISBN-10: 1-60138-046-1

Library of Congress Cataloging-in-Publication Data

Harris, Dianne C., 1952-
The complete guide to writing effective & award-winning grants: step-by-step instructions, with companion CD-ROM / by Dianne C. Harris.

p. cm.
Includes bibliographical references and index.
ISBN-13: 978-1-60138-046-3 (alk. paper)
ISBN-10: 1-60138-046-1 (alk. paper)
1. Proposal writing for grants. I. Title.

HG177.H37 2008
658.15'224--dc22
2007049116

INTERIOR LAYOUT DESIGN: Vickie Taylor • vtaylor@atlantic-pub.com

Printed in the United States

Printed on Recycled Paper

We recently lost our beloved pet "Bear," who was not only our best and dearest friend, but also the "Vice President of Sunshine" here at Atlantic Publishing. He did not receive a salary but worked tirelessly 24 hours a day to please his parents. Bear was a rescue dog that turned around and showered myself, my wife Sherri, his grandparents Jean, Bob, and Nancy and every person and animal he met (maybe not rabbits) with friendship and love. He made a lot of people smile every day.

We wanted you to know that a portion of the profits of this book will be donated to The Humane Society of the United States.

— *Douglas & Sherri Brown*

THE HUMANE SOCIETY OF THE UNITED STATES©

The human-animal bond is as old as human history. We cherish our animal companions for their unconditional affection and acceptance. We feel a thrill when we glimpse wild creatures in their natural habitat or in our own backyard.

Unfortunately, the human-animal bond has at times been weakened. Humans have exploited some animal species to the point of extinction.

The Humane Society of the United States makes a difference in the lives of animals here at home and worldwide. The HSUS is dedicated to creating a world where our relationship with animals is guided by compassion. We seek a truly humane society in which animals are respected for their intrinsic value and where the human-animal bond is strong.

Want to help animals? We have plenty of suggestions. Adopt a pet from a local shelter; join The Humane Society and be a part of our work to help companion animals and wildlife. You will be funding our educational, legislative, investigative, and outreach projects in the United States and across the globe.

Or perhaps you'd like to make a memorial donation in honor of a pet, friend or relative? You can through our Kindred Spirits program. If you'd like to contribute in a more structured way, our Planned Giving Office has suggestions about estate planning, annuities, and even gifts of stock that avoid capital gains taxes.

Maybe you have land that you would like to preserve as a lasting habitat for wildlife. Our Wildlife Land Trust can help you. Perhaps the land you want to share is a backyard — that's enough. Our Urban Wildlife Sanctuary Program will show you how to create a habitat for your wild neighbors.

So you see, it's easy to help animals, and The HSUS is here to help.

TABLE OF CONTENTS

CHAPTER 3: WHERE TO FIND GRANTS & TYPES OF GRANTS 57

FOREWORD

By Randall P. Fletcher

Preparing for an IRS audit or facing the dentist's drill sometimes pales in comparison to the process and pain involved in developing a grant application.

Regardless of the trauma grants may invoke, novice writers can develop grant applications as successfully as seasoned veterans. For all types of writers, grant writing is a dynamic process that involves higher-order thinking, organization, and fortitude. Many grant applications lay in trash cans or recycling carts or are reduced to shredded fragments because the would-be grant writer found the process far too difficult and abandoned the task weeks before the deadline.

Help has arrived. Nearly all grant writers, myself included, rely on good writing samples or models to help shape and cultivate ideas for our proposals. *The Complete Guide to Writing Effective and Award-Winning Grants* provides just that. In a step-by-step fashion, this valuable resource not only gives grant writers valuable information about the basics of grant writing, but also gives detailed case studies on what makes a successful application.

The art of grant writing is something that can be mastered by many. Being educated in how all the functions and aspects of grant research, application development, and grants administration work and how to use these tangible tools can transform you over time into a successful grant writer. Excellent grant writing skills can secure your organization or company the new levels of operating capital needed to start important programs, develop new innovations, and solve societal problems.

Much of the information contained in this comprehensive book can be found online, in print journals, and in grant writing organizational literature. However, to have all the needed skills, it is helpful to have hints and case study evidence bundled in one handy resource, especially if you are facing a deadline.

When I started writing grants almost 10 years ago, I learned the basics by reviewing grant applications that others had written. This gave me a keen sense of how a successful grant should be developed, from the opening sentence and the need statement, all the way to the final line of the budget narrative. The grant process is truly a trial-and-error experience. I have made my share of mistakes, and so will you. In the end, though, you will become a writer of multiple award-winning applications. It will happen, trust me.

Today, there are too few publications that provide information for all types and levels of grant writers. *The Complete Guide to Writing Effective and Award-Winning Grants* is now one of those few publications.

Randall P. Fletcher
President
Grant Professionals
205 East School Street
P.O. Box 81
Royal, IL 61871
www.grantprof.com
217-583-3023 or 217-721-9574

INTRODUCTION

Writing this book presented an opportunity to explain some important aspects of successful grant writing to people who are new to the task. There are many good volumes written about the basic format of a typical grant and lists of foundation and governmental grants available. Even though resources for the grant seeker are easily available, inexperienced writers may still feel intimidated by the writing process. Grant seekers that feel too busy to conduct the necessary research and coordination required for a grant funding campaign may unfortunately shortchange their programs by avoiding grant proposals. Sometimes a perplexed or overly extended group will decide it best to acquire the services of a professional grant writer, but the group may still have difficulty if it has little experience in the procurement and managing of professional services contracts. This book is designed to help you become an effective grant writer. You will learn how to determine your readiness to compete for grants, how to more efficiently hone in on the grant makers that are most likely to fund your project, how to organize the material needed for different types of grants; how to clearly write your grant proposal, how to use grant funds as a mechanism to accomplish your goals, and how to successfully manage your grant so that more funds will flow in the future.

I wanted to write this book because I have worked in the field of community development and regional planning for more than 18 years, with a specialty in writing grant applications and successful administration of grant-funded programs. I have served numerous clients, and they have all become personal and professional friends. But this book allows me to reach out to and help far more organizations and, indirectly, those they serve. I have had my share of happy successes and painful "learning experiences" in the writing and submission of proposals. I have also had the experience of having to administer and implement the programs that I so "skillfully" helped to conceptualize and communicate on the printed page, and, believe me, some ideas sound a lot better on paper. My own experiences are also enriched by the shared experiences of a network of professionals in similar positions who, over the years, have been my mentors, compatriots, and friends.

I have had my share of projects where I was unable to secure funding. When hopes are high, it is painful to work so hard and not achieve the funding so badly needed. In more than one instance the project missed basic thresholds. In one particularly embarrassing case I failed to note that a resolution adopting a market study was needed from the town's council. This was a failure at a number of steps. The team did not allow enough time to complete the survey work and was so rushed in putting together the market study that, by the time the requirements were reviewed, it was too late to get the resolution passed. The decision was made to submit the proposal, as it was to gain the benefit of commentary the reviewers would provide. This information, plus an entire year to get the resolution passed, ensured that the next submission would rank highly. I learned that it is possible to recover from a misstep, but the loss of a year's funding is still a big setback for a program.

Another form of disappointment came not in the writing of the proposal, but in the implementation once the funds had been secured. We had assembled a great team, a great idea, and a modest proposal. Still, after receiving the funds, the program was unable to get any qualified applicants for the assistance. Clearly we had not accurately assessed the feasibility of implementing the program within our target clientele. Before we try this program again, we will have to do more thorough investigations of how to reach that target audience and perhaps recruit additional partners for referring qualified applicants to us. The funder was agreeable and extended the grant period. A few clients were served, but we did not reach our program goals. The balance of the funds had to be returned to the grantor. Fortunately, the project overhead was provided "in-kind;" that is, by other sources. It would have been very difficult to repay funds spent on the overhead otherwise.

In occasions of the successful type, I have taken an unsuccessful application written by others and rewritten the application or in consultation suggested modifications to the proposed program, thus restructuring the project so that the next submission was indeed funded. Happily, my teams I and have always been able to learn, adjust, and make better repeat submissions as long as the applicant agencies did not give up. Each time this was done, the next proposal was better and our rate of success improved enormously. I hope in this book to share these lessons and insights.

Therefore, individuals and organizations should resolve to invest the necessary time and energy into learning to create successful grant proposals. Millions of dollars of grant funds go unclaimed every year because the right grant seeker did not approach the right foundation or did not convincingly present the proposal. It is a sad reality that there are so many problems in the world, but many great organizations are working to reduce suffering. Grant foundations have sincere missions to serve society in particular ways. A number of truly inspiring folks have done the work and founded networks of nonprofit, faith-based, and sometimes governmental programs to address problems found in their communities. A friend I will call KR is the Director of Community Development for a rural county in Ohio. Over the years, he has won millions in grants for home improvements and clean water that directly benefit the citizens of the county as well as funds to support businesses that develop the local economy. He once observed that he could look out any window on any day and see something that needed fixing in his community.

Yet these inspiring people and their programs often are unable to serve all the needs of those who apply to them without seeking additional grant funding. The national economy is forever in a state of fluctuation, sometimes rebounding, sometimes on the decline. Awareness is growing of increasing numbers of people living below the poverty line, even in middle-class suburbs. More than ever, organizations and individuals need to find and win those unclaimed grants and awards that are available to them. They owe it to those they serve and to those who work with them for change.

Even those who have been successful in the past in receiving grant support should continue to explore new grant sources and keep their proposal skills up to date. Once familiar grant sources may unexpectedly become less reliable. Individual funds may not provide the same level of support per award as provided in the past for a variety of reasons. Perhaps due to an internal administration issue, they may postpone making any grants while they reorganize. The endowments of grant making foundations may have suffered from downturns in the stock market or unfortunate investment choices. The generous outpouring of donations in response to the September 11, 2001 attacks, the Indonesian Tsunami of 2004, and hurricanes Katrina and Rita had the unfortunate effect of diverting donor cash from fund-raising for local causes. There is increasing competition for simultaneously shrinking federal grant supports as well. But new grant seekers should not be discouraged, as funds are available. Local causes are beginning to recover to their previous levels, and new foundations with new missions are formed each year. It means only that awards from better-known foundations may be more competitive due to their high visibility, while other opportunities are waiting to be discovered. All organizations should have some "Plan B" ideas of new sources to approach for funding, while others may have a critical need to look for new benefactors to expand their work.

One error made by members of grassroots organizations, individual grant seekers, or even small communities that want to get started, move to the next level, or to begin a new program or project, is to look for the services of a grant writer when the project is not yet ready for grant funding. Having conceived of a project idea, a prospective applicant believes a grant is a quick source of capital to acquire space, supplies, personnel, or other resources to jump start the operation. The client has heard that someone may be able to get the organization a grant. It is difficult to give a 30-second answer to the question of how long it takes to get a grant, given all the variables that would have to be considered. A professional writer will know fairly quickly if the project is not yet at a fundable stage. If time allows, the writer will at least meet with the grant seeker, listen to the pitch, and try to advise about the next steps the program should take to become fundable. With this book, hopeful grant seekers can learn step-by-step how to build and position their organization, develop strong programs, create effective proposals, and become successful at receiving grant awards, if they are ready to do a bit more work.

This book can save the grant seeker hundreds of dollars in writing fees and countless hours that might be wasted in ineffective proposal presentations. It will be the guide to accessing hundreds or thousands of dollars in grant support. First of all, no matter what level of accomplishment you have achieved to date, individuals and organizations are eligible for a number of scholarships, fellowships, and grant programs. Grants, unlike loans, do not have to be paid back. Each applicant must be able to demonstrate that he or she meets the criteria and stands out from a field of other applicants. Grant seekers that have passion for their work and are committed to their causes should be willing to invest time in obtaining skills and advice that will enable them to be more effective as organizations and increase their impact in their communities. Second of all, this book will help grant seekers evaluate the variables that apply to their situation and arrive at the answer to the questions, "What is the best grant for me/us?" and "How do I/we get one?" This book goes on to lead you through the post-grant award period: how to handle site visits from benefactors, how to prepare status and performance reports, and how to increase your likelihood of receiving more funds in the future.

This book will show you how to conduct a critical self-assessment of your organization's strengths, capacity, plans, or needs. This is the groundwork and most important first step. This self-evaluation will assist you in determining which grant makers provide the best match for their purposes and yours. You will be given leads to help you target your research to the most feasible opportunities, from the thousands of grants available, and find those best aligned with your particular needs and capacity. You will learn step-by-step how to organize your proposal and how to describe your project to a potential funder.

This book is organized following the typical step-by-step process of grant writing: from creating the structure of your new organization, forming your project idea, and locating the grant(s) from which you wish to request funds, to preparing and submitting your proposal and following through with the all-important post-grant award requirements. There is also a section on contingency plans if your effort is not successful and using that information to strengthen your next submission — a learning experience all its own.

Several chapters contain case studies or short examples obtained through interviews with successful grant writers and representatives of grant making organizations. These sources are also quoted throughout the text when their insights are most helpful. Each chapter is summarized with quick, easy-to-remember bullets of key points. Several sample forms and documents are assembled in the Appendix and available on the companion CD-ROM. In some chapters a case study may be revisited where it illustrates the focus of that chapter as well.

Section 1 of this book describes necessary preliminary steps to the writing of the grant application. Chapter 1: An Idea is Born and Chapter 2: It

Takes Earned Money To Get Free Money, are for the person or group that has just generated the idea for something they want to accomplish. The organization may have an idea that grants can help it with that goal. However, it needs the organizational structure, or strengthening of the small group or company, to fully develop and run a program. If these steps are missing, no amount of writing skill can overcome the funder's impression that you are not a good investment. Later, in the instructional chapters, Chapter 12 deals with writing the section of the grant that presents the qualifications of the applicant to receive a grant. Being able to write this qualifications section depends on having already built an organization as described in Chapters 1 and 2. The grant seeker that has a strong organization already, including governmental units, can likely skip ahead of Chapters 1 and 2 to the next chapters.

Chapter 3 elaborates on the types of grants available, eligibility categories, and where to find information about them. In brief, these categories are grants available only to nonprofit groups or educational institutions, grants available only to governmental agencies, and grants available only to individuals or companies. Chapter 4 examines the motivations of funders in providing their grants and how this relates to their review process. This knowledge will shape your decision to apply for a particular grant and the way a grant proposal might be presented. Chapter 5: Getting Organized provides some helpful hints for gathering your resources, making time, and putting your ideas down on paper. It includes some checklists, sample schedules, and writing tips.

Section 2: The Parts of a Grant Application presents in each chapter a key component of typical grant applications. They are presented in the usual order; although some funders may specify a somewhat different format, all these components will need to be presented in each proposal to stand out from other applicants.

Section 3 deals with the aftermath of receiving grant funds, otherwise known as "post-grant management." This is a critical period. The successful implementation of your program and appropriate documentation of the use of grant funds will be the single most critical factor in being able to return to a funder for future support. The Appendix contain some additional materials that may be useful: a proposal template using the instructions found throughout the book, useful Web sites, examples of some common forms, and a sample grant and grant application.

No matter what your past experience with preparing grant applications, this volume will be your companion in expanding your revenues and helping you to enhance your future success in winning grants. To me and others like me, there is no thrill quite like getting the phone call from a client saying the group just got word that the grant application I wrote for the organization was a winner. May your future be equally thrilling.

Section

First Things First

CHAPTER 1

AN IDEA IS BORN

CASE STUDY: HOPE FOR NEW LIFE PART 1

Our firm is a small consulting practice that assists small communities and nonprofit organizations with grant writing, grant administration, and planning projects. Over the years we established a solid reputation for successfully winning grant funding and excellent compliance in post-grant activities.

When our clients encounter a request for assistance that they do not know how to handle, they refer the potential applicant to us to see if we can help the applicant access special types of funding. Several years ago a gentleman called our firm to ask us to prepare a grant application for him. He represented the group that we will give the fictitious name "Hope for New Life" and wanted a multimillion dollar grant request from our city. He was referred to us by an employee of the city who clearly intended to deflect this person onto someone else. The caller had recently formed an organization that had not yet received its not-for-profit status from the Internal Revenue Service (IRS) and did not know that it needed to do so. However, a board of directors had been created, consisting of himself, his wife, and his uncle. They had a fairly reasonable-sounding idea to substantially reduce welfare in the city by providing job training, transportation assistance for the trainees, and childcare for the trainees. They had attempted one fund-raising event, a dance, and lost $127 on the effort. He had been encouraged by the warm reception of his ideas by one of our city council members, who had told him to bring in a well-drafted proposal and he could have the city's entire Community Development Block Grant (CDBG) allocation for that year. So that's what he wanted, the entire $9 million!

— Dianne Harris

WHO ARE YOU WRITING A GRANT APPLICATION FOR?

A grant writer might be freelance writer with a specialty in grant applications or a member of a larger consulting firm and might serve any type of grant seeking client. My firm was primarily a company concerned with community planning and development and the related grant programs, but it also worked with various nonprofit groups. However, I know engineering firms that prepare grant applications to obtain funding for projects they design for their clients. For example, they might help secure Environmental Protection Agency (EPA) funds for a town that needs to install new sanitary sewer lines. I have known of some legal firms that would assist a client, particularly local governments or nonprofits, in obtaining grants. I have met energetic teachers or employees of an organization that had great ideas for which there was no room in their employers' budgets to attempt implementation. These dedicated people sought out grant funds to purchase materials or equipment that enabled them to implement the new idea or program that benefited their employers' missions and perhaps did not benefit the grant writer directly at all. One public employee in a nearby community's utility department became fascinated with alternative energy, fuel cells in particular. He located and successfully applied for a grant to purchase a fuel cell generator for his town to use to generate some of its electricity while also allowing them to be a live demonstration of the technology for citizens and communities alike.

Many grant writers are employees of nonprofits, governments, and private organizations that already have a "full plate" of regular job responsibilities. Grant writing may be part of their regular duties, or it may be something additional that has been assigned to them on a one-time basis. When the organization chooses to not prepare the grant application with existing staff, it will seek the services of the various freelancers and consulting firms discussed previously. The following section presents some considerations of the choice to hire a grant writer.

Hiring a Grant Writer

Once you have selected a foundation or agency to submit your proposal or letter of intent to, you must designate the person who will actually write, compile, and submit your request. If a capable person exists in your organization, allow him or her to prepare the proposal.

An outside candidate may have to be brought up to speed about your organization, the program, and perhaps even the problem you seek to address before the writer can write well about you. This will require some investment of your time as well. If you can screen your candidates for one that has some background knowledge about you and your field, it will reduce the time involved in this orientation.

In some cases, either the internal candidates lack the confidence or time to properly research and prepare the application. When that happens, the organization may seek outside help with researching and writing the grant application. If that person can be enticed to work as a volunteer, that is even better. However, if you approach a professional writer or consultant, be prepared to discuss the needed services in detail and to be charged the usual rate. Such arrangements should be outlined in a written service agreement. A service agreement will describe the work to be done (or specific grants to write), an agreed on fee for the service, and any relevant certifications and details as to responsibilities for sharing information, preparation of the grant application, and expenses of making the submission.

> **TIP:** *It is best and least expensive if the client researches available grants and instructs the hired writer about which foundations should be approached. In the event the client wants the hired writer to do the research, there should be a fixed time for conducting the research, an agreed format for presenting findings, and a clear method of compensation for this time.*

Most grants do not allow for reimbursement of costs incurred prior to the receipt of the grant. Do not assume that you can pay a grant writer with some of the grant proceeds, unless specifically advised that this would be an eligible cost.

Your grant writer needs to have a track record of working well under pressure, be someone you are comfortable working with and sharing somewhat sensitive information, and must demonstrate the ability to meet deadlines. The writer needs to be a little bit of a salesperson and be able to translate possibly technical terms into language that is clear and easily understood by a reviewer that may not be an expert in your field. Still, this does not need to be someone with a creative writing or marketing degree. I have found that the most effective grant proposals come from organizations that have thoroughly planned a great program and completely thought out the details of establishing and running that program. Then the story almost tells itself.

At the end of Chapter 2, there are samples of a letter requesting a written cost quote from prospective grant writers. Just as when procuring services for any major investment, it is best to obtain quotes from at least three bidders for this service. Following the letter is a sample of a typical contract for services. This is for illustration purposes. All contracts and legal documents should be reviewed by your attorney for compliance with your state laws.

The Applicant

The wise grant writer will assess the applicant and what it expects you to accomplish before accepting an assignment. The first step in assessing the applicant is determining the organization's legal status, which largely determines what types of grant funding it will be eligible for. In reality, the first step in preparing a grant application occurs before you, the writer, gets involved with thinking about available grants. A grant seeker must first be an actual, bona fide entity. If it is an organization, it must have a duly constituted board of directors, a set of bylaws, a letter showing IRS tax status, and a bank account. If it is a nonprofit, many granting agencies will want evidence of its tax-exempt status, or it can partner with a sponsoring organization that holds a tax-exempt certificate. If the grant seeker is an individual or for-profit business, it may be necessary to produce tax returns, proof of residency, and other evidence of compliance with various laws to qualify for certain grants.

The first order of business for a grant writer must therefore be understanding the applicant's status (individual, business, nonprofit, for-profit, governmental) and to be sure sufficient documentation exists to prove its status and primary functions and activities. In the case of an individual applicant for scholarships, fellowships, or special grants, there must be some demonstrable ability in his or her field, supported by a portfolio of work and perhaps awards and other recognition of ability by experts in the discipline. Agencies that provide grants want to be sure they have made a good investment in a well-designed program with strong leadership or an individual that shows talent and potential for success. Funders want to be able to show, in concrete terms, that their money has contributed to the improvement of the world in some way. Several of the subjects introduced in this chapter will be presented in greater detail in the step-by-step instructions for writing an effective grant proposal in later chapters.

The grant writer must develop an understanding of the targeted problem or objective for use of the funds and a sense of the applicant's mission to alleviate the problem. The grant writer needs to know that his or her client or project is created or supported by a group of like-minded and knowledgeable people. If the problem is too big for a single individual to work on, he or she should develop an organization of creative people to share the responsibility for solving this problem. The grant writer may need to assist the prospective applicant in making this determination and in seeking out visionary partners and convincing them of the need to participate with this organization or project. The first proposal anyone creates is the effort to recruit these potential board members, volunteers, and supporters as partners in achieving the mission. An appeal to them for their services will incorporate the steps of a successful grant application, just less formally delivered. If there is a recognized need for board members, volunteers, and other supporters who have deep connections in the philanthropic community and who may not be among your personal acquaintances, a more formal "pitch" to gain audience with them and recruit them to serve with you may be needed. This pitch may sound very much like a grant proposal and should be carefully constructed and rehearsed. Having all the same information needed for a grant proposal will assure them that this is a professional and worthy individual or organization with which to associate.

These are the most basic resources to gather when you and your applicant are beginning to function as a team. From that basic capacity, the next step is to work toward accomplishments that further prove your ability to succeed and thus attract more partners, volunteers, and donations. The ability to recruit quality board members and volunteers is an indication of community support for your ideas, of capability to communicate the targeted problem to the public, and of ability to organize and manage volunteers and projects. These steps of building support for a project, generating volunteers and board members, and reaching the first achievements are done by the applicant prior to engaging a grant writer. If the grant writer finds during the assessment of the applicant that more work in these or other areas will be necessary to make the applicant competitive for funding, it is honorable to point out the deficiencies before agreeing to accept money for writing a grant application. A writer may be able to help the group with the capacity-building stage or perhaps even to find some startup or capacity-building grants. It is important to clearly outline this expanded scope of work and come to a fair agreement for payment for these additional services.

Hope for New Life, the grant seeker in Case Study #1, identified a community need and formulated an idea that addressed several of the problems an unemployed single parent might find in trying to join the work force. However, from there the organization Hope for New Life seemed not to have any formal structure, and there seemed to be no effort to bring in board members or volunteers with credentials or special knowledge of these areas. More important, it seemed resistant to the suggestion, making the organization appear to be little more than a scam.

If the grant writer finds that organization or other applicant has already established its legal status and some proficiency in its field and has gotten past the startup phase, the next thing to look for is a clearly stated vision, a dream of a better future, and a mission for the entity that helps to fulfill that dream. This is true for any applicant, individual, for-profit, nonprofit, or even government. Goals should be clearly articulated to everyone in the organization, from the board to the staff and even the volunteers. In the case of an individual, or a for-profit business, its clientele and patrons should understand the vision associated with the applicant's craft.

Author Stephen Covey has written that all people, families, and organizations are more effective when they have taken time to express a vision and mission for their lives or organization. The mission clearly states the role the individual or organization will have in the community, how it intends to carry out its work, and why. Any projects or programs it undertakes should clearly relate to the accomplishment of this mission. The grant writer must convey that sense of vision and the mission of the organization to the targeted funder in each component of a proposal: the proposal summary, the organization description, and the needs statement. The board members of Hope for New Life had an idea of what their mission was but did not have the training in strategic planning to articulate that mission. Furthermore, it was starting with only the roughest outline of what it intended to do and had not begun to research the methodology and requirements directly related to the activities or any kind of business or action plan. It wanted to start with the money and then figure out how to spend it. That is not an approach that will be successful in gaining grant funding.

The grant writer may have to steer the new group toward future success by showing it how it must go through the steps of formally establishing its organizational structure, with by-laws and rules of order. As mentioned previously, the grant writer, if finding the group has not done this, may assist in the finding of a partner. It must rely on the support of an established organization or individual to act as the actual grantee that will be willing to pass along some of the funds on a sub-grantee basis. These types of partnerships can be an effective way to quickly get into action. A group needs to establish a bank account, vote in officers, designate committees, and begin application for a determination of tax status. An organization needs a not-for-profit status, a 501(c)(3), to be able to receive grants resulting from tax deductible donations. Other types of nonprofits eligible to receive tax deductible donations are fraternal organizations as described in Section 501(c)(8) or 501(c)(10), cemetery companies as described in Section 501(c)(13), volunteer fire departments under Section 501(c)(4), and veterans' organizations under 501(c)(4) or 501(c)(19) of the Internal Revenue Service code. There are several other types of nonprofits under the U.S. Tax Code that are not eligible to receive tax-deductible donations, such as labor organizations under Section 501(c)(5), business leagues and trade associations under 501(c)(6), agricultural/horticultural organizations under Section 501(c)(5), or political organizations under Section 527.

The company or organization will also need to register with the state agency that oversees business registrations and activities and possibly obtain state or local licenses, zoning approvals, and permits for the activities it will be undertaking. This is also true for individuals who have chosen to establish a business identity for themselves for taxing or liability protection purposes. For example, not-for-profit child care providers may need health and fire code inspections prior to opening. The state may have regulations as to the qualifications of the workers and limits on the ratios of children under the care of each caregiver. Workers may need to pass strict background checks, and as an employer, your group will be subject to labor laws, enforcement of child support withholding, and even making sure your employees are living and working in the country legally. Check with authorities to find out if the proposed organization will require some of these permits or others.

Organizations that are not as formally organized are often referred to as "grassroots" organizations. The grassroots organization is very important to community functions and conducts its work at the local level. Grassroots organizations have access to highly specific forms of grant funding, through local foundations that know its leaders and support its mission. In the case study of what not to do, Hope for New Life had not created a legal or tax entity and, since it was organized by members of the same family, had not felt it necessary to create a charter or by-laws. It is extremely shortsighted and dangerous to the health of the organization to assume that everyone has the same clear understanding of an organization's purpose, what rules should apply, and what duties are the responsibility of whom within the organization. Hope for New Life wanted to skip the process of organizing and the grassroots growth phase, thinking it could go right to the "big bucks." Effective organizations take appropriate actions and win the grants.

ASSESSING CAPABILITY

Formally organized not-for-profits, having achieved that status and formulated a project or program idea, should honestly evaluate their capacity to create and run a new program. They must be professional in their ability to efficiently and effectively manage and use the funds they seek. Although some readers represent well-established organizations and programs, some organizations are at different stages of their development, perhaps in their "infant," conceptual stages. The grant seekers of Hope for New Life may have honestly believed that they were smart people and would be able to handle the almost $9 million they intended to take away from well-established organizations. However, they had no prior business or not-for-profit experience of any kind and no staff. Even the cleverest wordsmith could not make a case for their capacity, let alone prove it. They further demonstrated a lack of understanding as to how grants are awarded and managed by failing to recognize that the city had many years of experience funding social service and construction projects from the Community Development Block Grant (CDBG) program (discussed more in Chapter 3). The city's review process included a review team to evaluate proposals and how they fit in with stated city priorities. The council person sat on this committee but most likely would never have supported the idea that urgent infrastructure improvements in low income neighborhoods or that healthcare and other services for low income people should be left out of a coming year's budget in favor of any one single organization. It is important to be realistic with requests.

To be sure, startups and grassroots organizations do have access to funding. These programs are often called "seed money" grants. Seed money grants are not large but are intended to help an idea "grow." However, most funding organizations are looking for some level of expertise and more experience as the amount of the request or the complexity of the project increases. Before the grant seeker can hope to attract large grant awards, it must be well established and have its tax status accurately determined. Many grant awards (but not all) are restricted to nonprofits that have the exemption certificate, known as the 501(c)(3) from the Internal Revenue Service (IRS) in place and be able to demonstrate a system of financial controls set up according to standard accounting processes. The IRS provides guidance about the qualifications and filing procedures for the appropriate tax exemption on its Web site, **www.irs.gov**. Many organizations obtain legal assistance with this step, but it is not absolutely necessary. In addition, the process of getting tax-exempt status can take a year or more, and there are filing fees that will need to be covered by some of your early fund-raising efforts.

Individual applicants, for example artists and writers, to demonstrate their capability should select their best work to create a portfolio that reflects the interests and genres that they profess to be working in. They may need to be able to explain the philosophies, inspirations, materials, and techniques that influence their creative processes.

The structure of the board of directors or board of trustees will be scrutinized. Some foundations want to see that the board members bring expertise in a range of matters, such as law, banking, and finance; the area of activity (such as social change or environmental protection); or perhaps that the board has representation from a diverse group of community stakeholders. Most important, the board members should be committed to advancing the mission of the organization and to providing resources and funds necessary to accomplish the mission. Projects undertaken should be true to that mission and directly address the needs identified. In our case study, the board consisted only of three individuals who were lacking in experience, knowledge, and commitment. Their lack of commitment was demonstrated in that they had done nothing to gain the necessary expertise and knowledge in the areas that they hoped to work in; they had not even researched the state's requirements for operation of a daycare center. They knew nothing about how to set up an approved job training site and program and had not even tried to work out the rudiments of a budget.

If not already in place, the organization must implement a strategy to generate some of its own non-grant source funds. This is necessary to cover some of the early startup costs, as well as ongoing basic operations. The ability to successfully raise capital shows funders that the organization's work and reputation in the community are valued and supported. Successful fund-raising also demonstrates an ability to organize and carry out a project. Unlike the man from Hope For New Life, do not lock in on a single grant source because it seems to have funds available. It will be more effective to seek support from several foundations, as it minimizes the risk and investment for each. Effective organizations build partnerships that blend several sources of funds and will have to devote a significant amount of time to fund-raising activities. Recruiting volunteers to participate is valuable for these efforts, as well as for providing direct service to project clients. An organization can expect to raise funds through sponsorship of events, direct appeals for donations, or entrepreneurial activities, such as sales of goods and services. Seldom will a foundation source agree to be the sole supply of funds. Frequently a grant program requires matching funds, or in-kind donations or services, to provide for a portion of the project costs. The case study group believed that its lack of success with fund-raising only made a stronger case for the need for grant support. It were wrong. In the case of grant requests it is true that "nothing succeeds like success."

When selecting projects and programs, an organization needs to establish priorities. There is a limit to the amount of time an organization can dedicate to each interest. A rule of thumb is to not try to work on more than three completely new projects at a time, depending on size. The grant seeker must decide what he or she most wants to do, what other resources and partners can be invited to join together, how much additional funding is needed (the gap), and then and only then, who best to ask for this additional support.

Partnerships and Networking

As forming the organization and day-to-day business proceed, the organization cannot operate in isolation from the rest of its community. Clients may be interacting with other service providers for some of their other needs. Donors may be supporting other service providers. Sometimes additional expertise is needed to deliver a service effectively. It is important to have a network of others to share knowledge and provide encouragement and referrals.

Seek out ways to connect with others in the community besides clients served and those who financially support the project. Join in nonprofit councils, be a leader in professional affiliation organizations, and volunteer for other civic boards. The contacts and friendships made through networking will have multiple long-term benefits. In casual contact, there is an opportunity to share "war stories" and insights with others who have had similar experiences. There is an opportunity to learn of other organizations, their programs, challenges, and solutions, and to share yours. It will help to decrease the sense of isolation and being "stuck." Professional affiliations provide the opportunity to connect with new practices and a group of peers with which to examine new theories, as well as practical advice about administration and personnel issues. You will develop contacts at higher levels of government, organizations, and corporations that can help shorten the path to assistance or provide new program ideas when you need them.

Networking does require a commitment of time and budget to attend conferences, luncheons, and other events. It also involves time to develop a relationship with members of the network and to make occasional contacts outside of the group activities. Some organizations make these available inexpensively, and others may be quite costly. Almost every town now has a Chamber of Commerce or a business networking group. These local organizations can help to link you to the business community and potential benefactors and are affordable. An important way to get recognition for your program or project is to volunteer to work on an event for the group, or volunteer to host a get-together for the group at your facility if you have space. Another way you can grow your network and gain recognition is to volunteer to serve on a church or youth group committee or a local governmental committee or commission, for example, the local zoning board or parks board, or even the community parade organizers. As you gain recognition, you will gradually be invited to move on to other committees and boards and will have many opportunities to spread information about your programs or projects. Networking involves giving as well as being on the receiving end of a relationship.

That said, another lesson to be learned from the experience of the ambitious board of Hope for New Life concerns the impact of networking and political support. It is truly helpful to develop relationships with funders and with your elected officials. However, politicians have less influence over major grant programs than one might think. They have a lot of constituents and many established priorities. Beware of promises with big "ifs" attached or that seem too good to be true. It takes more than one short conversation to establish a working relationship with anyone whose support is being sought. It is best to forge a relationship based on mutual interests before broaching the subject of financial support. Keep the organization visible, active, and involved with civic life. Attend meetings or volunteer for citizen committees or community roundtables. These are a part of networking. By being more visible to others, an organization will enhance its credibility.

All these organizations may be able to recommend grant fund sources or potential major donors. Others in the network may possibly provide an introduction to a staff member or member of the board of the funding source. Personal contact will provide you with the opportunity to develop in-depth knowledge of a funding organization and the great work it does, increasing chances of a favorable review for a subsequent grant proposal. This opportunity to network is crucial when you hope to gain access to foundations that do not use open application processes. They choose to control the number and type of proposals they receive by funding only proposals from those to whom they have issued an invitation to apply.

A public relations strategy can also help reach out to potential donors and potential partners and can help funders become aware of the organization and its work. It is possible to hire firms that specialize in creating public relations campaigns, but many business assistance publications, Web sites, and organizations offer "shoestring" ideas for inexpensive outreach actions. Every communication that comes from your program can help to raise its awareness and enhance its image. Web sites are almost expected avenues to distribute a message to anyone curious about your work. Blogs, a special form of interactive Web site, are increasingly popular as well. Inexpensive Web site and blog hosting are more available now, and chances are that someone with basic Web design skills can be recruited to donate some services. Production of a mailed newsletter is still a widely used way to maintain communications with donors, existing and potential, as well as partners, and is useful to reach those that are not yet regular users of the

Internet or computers. E-mail is an inexpensive way to distribute newsletters to anyone that would like to be on a distribution list. However, be careful to avoid sending junk e-mail. Allow the recipient to remove him or herself from the distribution list.

In addition to information about your organization/company, activities, calendars, and upcoming events, it is useful to post and distribute the annual report online, directly to donors, and to libraries. The traditional media of newspapers, radio, and television still provide inexpensive public relations or even paid advertising. Use free public service announcements opportunities or community bulletin boards to publish upcoming meeting and event notices. Invite reporters to cover meetings and events, or send press releases announcing new programs, awards (including successful grant awards), new board members and staff, and more. Other low cost options might include participating in community events with booths, floats, and raffles. Imprinted items such as pens and note pads make inexpensive items that can be handed out at events and are sure to be used and keep your program recognized. The simplest of these is a good supply of business cards. Thanks to new technologies, promo items can have significant visual impact and contain tidbits of useful information, such as a local sports team's schedule, and are relatively inexpensive for large-scale distribution. Attach them to everything that goes out of your office, use them at networking events and conferences, and ask people to contact you. Be on the look out for venues that are low cost or free and will give you needed exposure to potential donors or target organizations. Be creative in the venue and in the method of participation. Highlight positive messages and accomplishments.

The network of resources you develop can also become more active partners in a program. Others may already be providing a service that would integrate well into an envisioned comprehensive service package. It is possible to work out shared duties in an expanded program, with them doing what they know. Or they may be a resource for assisting the launching of a service if it is not practical for them to provide it. They can be a critical link to funds that can flow through an organization only with their particular makeup or mission. Using partners in a program can help broaden the impact of the effort and create benefits that are greater than the sum of the parts.

As one might guess regarding Hope For New Life, we did not write that application for $9 million or for any amount. We did, however, review the situation and explain what the group needed to do to increase its chance of getting any funds, and we gave it some valuable free advice on how to get started and put first things first. It would be nice to say that the group took that advice and has grown into a successful organization, but it did not. Neither did it affiliate with any other like-minded organization.

Heading up a not-for-profit, like being an entrepreneur, is not a way of life that is best for everyone, and although many opportunities exist for a significant amount of grant support, there are thresholds. It can be hard work. But just as operating a business or a not-for-profit organization can be the culmination of a dream, dreams take nurturing, devotion, and work. Now that the basics of starting an organization and identifying a project activity have been reviewed, let us go through the steps and the hard but rewarding work of researching available grants, preparing grant applications, and letters of interest.

CHAPTER SUMMARY

- Before the grant request, build a strong organization.
- Have the dream firmly envisioned.
- Recruit committed, quality board members and volunteers.
- Clearly state the mission.

- Begin non-grant fund-raising.
- Establish legal and tax relationships.
- Set priorities.
- Design a project.
- Begin networking.
- Use a public relations strategy.
- Go after your share of the millions of dollars of grants that are available.

CHAPTER 2

IT TAKES EARNED MONEY TO GET FREE MONEY

CASE STUDY: KR

KR is the Community Development Director for a rural Midwestern county. He has secured $3 million in grants for this year alone. He said, "There's lots of money out there and available. It's 90 percent perspiration and only 10 percent inspiration.

"The funders hold up the hoops, and you jump through them. Contact them and establish a rapport, get the hints, then use them. And I never submit an application without making some contact to the agency first. Jump through all the hoops. Sometimes it seems like the life of a circus dog; if you jump through enough hoops, someone will throw you a biscuit. It's an open-book test. They tell you exactly what they want, what the criteria are, how it will be scored; you don't have to be a brain surgeon to get the funding."

— KR

This chapter will provide you with an overview of the grant writing process from the perspective of grants as one of several streams of income available to a nonprofit organization, unit of government, or an individual. It explains that you will not depend entirely on grants to accomplish your mission and why. The importance of approaching funders that would be inclined to support a project is introduced.

Even though millions of dollars of grant funds go unclaimed each year, grant makers are not necessarily desperate to find takers for their funds. It requires hard work to research grant makers, develop a project idea, and prepare an effective grant proposal. Of course there is the time needed to actually write the proposal, edit the work, and provide thorough documentation of needs and costs, as will be outlined in this book. But the organization, or individual, must demonstrate that it is hard at work on its mission, accomplishing its goals, and receiving money from multiple sources.

Most granting agencies expect that grants, at least their grants, will not be the only source of income for an organization to implement its projects and carry out its programs. There are a few reasons for this approach. As stated in Chapter 1, an organization's success in recruiting volunteers and soliciting donations is one of the best indications of the wider community's support for the organization and the community's agreement with the need for this solution. The grant foundation may be learning of the applicant for the very first time. Community support shows that those nearest to the applicant, and who know it best, have confidence in its abilities and reliability and have the same priorities. In the grant world, the old saying is true that "money attracts more money."

Foundations want to see that, while successfully raising funds, the organization is effectively setting and following budgets, adhering to good accounting practices, and receiving favorable audit reports. Their donors trust them to make good decisions in awarding grants with beneficial impacts. A demonstrated pattern of responsible financial practices demonstrates the capability to be good stewards of the investments. Grantors have goals, and grantees function as their partners in realizing those goals. As any business person would, they are going to closely examine the credentials and work ethic of any potential partner.

Details on conducting other non-grant fund-raising efforts are addressed in other volumes that explain how to successfully run a nonprofit organization. But the most basic example is the direct appeal for donations, whether by phone, mail, door-to-door solicitations, or other media. Some organizations are using the Internet to appeal to prior donors and enhance their success through year-round distribution of information about their programs and successes, particularly in the newsletter format. Many not-for-profits use special software to track donor contributions, not only for tax reporting purposes, but to analyze the segment of the community where their support has been strongest and whether certain types of appeals and fund-raising activities are more cost-effective than others. Guidance on available software can be found from **www.groundspring.org** or from the Foundation Center (**www.fdncenter.org**).

> **TIP:** *Acquire and use as many technology tools as possible to ease project tracking and to produce documents, promotional material, and status reports more efficiently. It will pay off in the capacity you gain to compile and distribute information and data easily and at great cost savings.*

Frequently one or more events may be used as a vehicle for raising community awareness of a problem and the organization's services, providing an opportunity for community entertainment while also raising funds. Examples include arts and crafts fairs, holiday parades, sports tournaments, various types of races, and annual banquets. Participants pay an entry fee, which covers event expenses and an additional amount that goes to the organization. Some events lend themselves to sales of admission for the public to attend. Recruiting sponsors for the event, or in-kind donation of space, food, advertising, and exhibition materials, helps to defray expenses and increase the actual proceeds generated by the event. Grants and donations can even be found to help with the costs of organizing or publicizing such an event. Often these events are of such high quality that they are recreated annually and are greatly anticipated by the public. One example is the annual Dispatch Charities Home and Garden

Show in Columbus, Ohio. The Dispatch Publishing Company (best known for the local daily newspaper in Columbus) is the main sponsor of the show. In addition to a trade show with booths set up by all manner of companies in home improvement, decorating, landscape design, garden, and home entertainment products and services, the show's biggest draw are the dozen or more fully created custom home landscapes for attendees to walk through, with water features, blooming plants, and trees. Held while snow is still on the ground, the event is a popular winter escape, inspiring attendees to think about improvements in their own homes and gardens and linking them with providers of the latest innovations. With all the landscapes and materials donated by sponsors, the admission fees and booth fees for the two-week event are dedicated to the Dispatch Charities Foundation and its grants awarded in the community.

Similarly, an organization might find a signature product to sell at a percentage markup to benefit the organization. T-shirts that cleverly advertise organizations abound. One of the best-known examples is the Girl Scout® cookie. Another is the Breast Cancer Awareness pink ribbon campaign. This campaign has expanded and demonstrates a variation in which corporate partners produce their own product lines, adapt the pink ribbon symbol to their product, and donate a portion of all sales to the not-for-profit cause. This campaign spread from jewelry and accessories to many clothing lines and can now be found on the packaging of a number of popular food products such as Campbell's® soups. The partner organization's contribution includes taking care of the distribution of the item, contributing to the marketing of the campaign, tallying the sales, and providing a single-point donor for the nonprofit instead of thousands of tiny donations.

Some not-for-profits take an even bigger step into the realm of entrepreneurialism. For example, many groups concerned with providing adequate housing for low income families and preventing homelessness find themselves in the business of building and renovating homes, acting as developers, landlords, and social service coordinators in the process. They are able to sell or rent the homes at a lower cost than a similar home in the for-profit market, keeping the costs affordable for their target groups and generating proceeds that help to maintain the organization and its administrative functions. One example is the Miracet Development Corporation, which has grown through the leveraging of government grants to build new single-family homes to sell to low income, working families. The proceeds from the sales sustain the organization while the grants defray construction costs to keep the homes affordable. By increasing home ownership in their neighborhoods and providing a range of services, such as tutoring and job search assistance, they are helping to improve families' abilities to gain greater economic stability.

Such activities require varying levels of time and investment of resources to set up and run, independent of the charitable work of the organization. It is easier to justify the time and effort when there is a direct relationship between the mission of the organization and the product.

Yet another particularly effective way to raise funds is the selling of an organization's excess time as services. Services that a nonprofit might sell as an income-generating venture include sales of a book or other publication, consulting services, fee-based training, organizational development programs, and even grant writing for others. The nonprofit can increase its visibility as an expert in its field, provide the community a benefit by sharing its expertise with others, help others meet continuing education requirements for their field, and help its bottom line, all at the same time. Some organizations get into this type of activity as they attempt to find a productive activity for the staff they already have. Often "think tank" type nonprofits, such as institutes and affiliates of colleges and universities, engage in this type of fund-raising. The Ohio State University Extension Services are particularly active in these enterprises. Though their primary mission is to promote agriculture and home-based technologies, the Extension Service serves economic and community development needs in rural Ohio, as well as increasing skills and knowledge of landscape horticulture in urban areas. The various county branches may provide competitively priced services such as grant writing for a local organization or government, or even grant administration services. Each branch provides a customized set of services and programs based on the needs of its service area. Branches often can be hired to provide strategic planning workshops or other community events for local nonprofits and small local governments to help enhance the professional administration of public entities. Their fees are often less than what would be paid to a for-profit professional consultant, and the fees help to support and grow their programs as a public service and nonprofit agency.

Why go through all this? Why can an organization not just focus on grants? First of all, there is not as much money available for startup organizations as there is for established ones. That means there must be a way to cover those initial startup expenses, such as filing fees with the IRS for determination of nonprofit status, stationery, meeting space, and telephones. Even if these products and services are donated, that is a form of successful fund-raising. Second of all, a grant program will focus on the cost of delivering just one activity, not the entire operational and capital expenses. Other sources will be needed to cover the rest of the budget or to engage in additional program activities. The ability to raise these funds and manage programs will demonstrate the level of professionalism that makes grant makers want to invest.

Grant makers want to know their money will go to "work" quickly and efficiently for the purposes they wish to support. Therefore, if the grant seeker is in a startup or building phase, the best grant sources will be funds dedicated to startup or expansion activities. It is not wise to create a charitable program solely because funds seem to be available for it or as an avenue to pay for the building the organization in other ways. There may not be enough money from a single grant to do both. But this can be an effective strategy as long as the program is a good fit with the organizational mission, there is a demonstrable need, and if enough resources can be generated to run a successful program. If more staff or larger facilities are needed to start a new program, those costs should be clearly identified to the foundation that you approach (more on that later). Last, and of utmost importance, most foundations do not provide repeated funding for the same activity to the same organization year after year. Unless a one-time activity is being proposed, a mechanism must be created to sustain the program, one that has a secure source of funding into the future. One-time activities are viable efforts and might include targeted responses to a unique situation, such as a disaster, or perhaps a demonstration program in which the intent is to prove that a program approach can be effective. The demonstration program can be used to provide information that will make the program idea more fundable on a larger scale in the future or to demonstrate to other organizations how the activity can be replicated in their communities.

For example, a small city I once worked for was interested in obtaining major funding for grants to dozens of downtown businesses to make façade upgrades in the town. Although unable to meet all the program thresholds at the time, for a single year it directed $25,000 of its annual Community Development Block Grant to do two projects as a demonstration program. The threshold criteria were not a factor in this case. The demonstration projects showed community leaders the impact the program could have, and they quickly decided to pass the necessary legislation in support of the larger program the following year. In addition, the community could point out in its application that it now had experience with this type of program and a waiting list of businesses that wanted to participate. This greatly increased its competitiveness for the larger grant, and it was successful in obtaining the funds and implementing the program.

Some grant programs are created specifically to support the creation of projects that demonstrate and disseminate innovation in specific fields, especially in education and therapeutic fields. In 1992 the U.S.

Administration on Aging created the Alzheimer's Disease Demonstration Grant, a matching grant whose purpose was to promote innovative regimens of care for Alzheimer's patients and their caregivers. For more than 15 years the methods and results of funded programs would be measured and distributed throughout the care community so that methods found to be effective under various circumstances could be quickly learned and adopted by others.

All these activities involve a lot of work and a lot of time. These are investments that enable an organization or individual to realize a vision. These are investments that an organization or individual must make to prove that the project or program is worthy of additional support from foundations and agencies. They may have little knowledge of the grant seeker's abilities, and the proposal must be able to demonstrate programmatic or organizational strengths as clearly as the case for the need for, and value of, the activities planned for funding.

CHAPTER SUMMARY

- Grant work is a valuable part of any fund-raising strategy.
- Grants are free but not easy.
- Drafting the proposal for funds is work.
- Fund-raising is work.
- Examples of other fund-raising:
    - Donations of time, materials, and money
    - Events
    - Selling merchandise

   ° Entrepreneurial

   ° Selling your expertise and services

- Other fund-raising is necessary:

   ° For startup funds

   ° For program sustainability

   ° To establish position as the best recipient for the grants desired

SAMPLE REQUEST FOR PROPOSALS
GRANT WRITING SERVICES

FROM:

Towne Sports, Inc.
c/o Mary Jones
2001 Ashtown Rd.
Columbia, OH 43200
Phone: 555-555-5555
Fax: 555-555-5556

Dear Prospective Service Provider:

The board of trustees of Towne Sports, Inc., the leading provider of organized sports programming for youth aged 13-17 in Columbia, is requesting proposals for grant writing activities. Towne Sports, Inc. has identified a foundation from which to apply for funding for the purpose of replacing the surface of the outdoor running track owned by Towne Sports on 2001 Ashtown Road.

The board is soliciting proposals from several service providers and reserves the right to negotiate the details of the final contract with the provider deemed most qualified to undertake this project or to not accept any of the proposals received.

The proposal should address at a minimum: 1) the provider's statement of qualifications and experience with similar work, 2) at least three client references, describing the work performed and a client reference and contact information, 3) a project schedule outlining project milestones, 4) a cost proposal detailing project fees and expected expenses.

SAMPLE REQUEST FOR PROPOSALS GRANT WRITING SERVICES

The proposal shall consist of no more than five pages secured by only one staple in the upper left corner. No other form of binding, please. Please submit five copies of the proposal to Mary Jones at the address above, no later than 4:30 p.m., January 15, 2005. The board will review the proposals and announce its selection at the next meeting of the board, January 22, 2005. Work will be expected to begin no later than January 28.

Thank you for your interest.

Sincerely,

Mary Jones, Administrative Assistant
Towne Sports, Inc.

SAMPLE CONTRACT

Agreement To Provide Professional Services

Consultant: Great Company, LLC

Client: Towne Sports, Inc.

This Agreement is effective as of the 17th day of January, 2005, by and between Great Company, LLC, a limited liability corporation existing under the laws of the State of Ohio, also referred to as "The Consultant" and "Towne Sports, Inc." also referred to as "Client."

Part 1. Description of Services

The Consultant agrees to provide the professional services specified as follows:

1. Research guidelines for grant applications from the SportsShoe Foundation.

2. Prepare a complete grant application for the SportsShoe Foundation Small Town Sports Program.

3. Submit the complete grant application to the foundation on or before the due date, in the format and number of copies designated by the foundation.

SAMPLE CONTRACT

4. Provide one review copy of the grant guidelines and the final application to the Executive Director of Towne Sports, Inc. at the address given below, one week prior to submission to the foundation.

Part 2. Time of Performance

The Consultant is to commence work no later than January 28, 2005 and complete the project prior to March 15, 2005.

Part 3. Client Responsibilities

1. The Client will cooperate with the Consultant by making all available information pertinent to the project.

2. Provide working space at the Client's offices for gathering documentation and duplication of materials for the final grant submission.

3. Provide other support to the Consultant if mutually agreed upon in order to successfully complete the grant application.

4. Promptly give written notice to the Consultant whenever the Client becomes aware of a defect in the project.

Part 4. Consultant Responsibilities

1. The Consultant will perform all activities necessary to complete and submit the application on or before the due date.

2. The Consultant will maintain strict confidentiality in relations with all parties regarding the Client's proprietary information and regarding any other confidential information obtained in the carrying out of this project.

3. Promptly give written notice to the Client whenever the Consultant becomes aware of any fault or defect in the project.

4. Upon completion of the project, return to the Client all documents used in and pertaining to the project.

Part 5. Compensation

The Client shall remit payment for services based upon hourly costs and

SAMPLE CONTRACT

reimbursable expenses in accordance with the cost of services portion of the scope of work. However, the total cost to perform that portion of the scope of work attributable to the Client shall be $ 1,000 for project services and reimbursement of expenses at cost.

Part 6. Payment Schedule

The Consultant will submit a single invoice to the Client for services rendered at the end of the project, and the Client agrees to remit compensation within thirty (30) days of receipt of invoice.

Part 7. Termination

The Client may cancel or terminate this Agreement for any reason upon written notice to the Consultant. Upon termination, the Client agrees to pay the Consultant for all work completed under this Agreement through the date of termination.

Part 8. Amendments

The Client may request changes in the scope of work to be performed by the Consultant under this Agreement. Mutually agreed changes by and between the Client and the Consultant will be attached by written amendment to this Agreement.

Part 9. State Law

The laws of the State of Ohio shall govern this Agreement.

Part 10. Liability

The Client shall indemnify and hold harmless the Consultant and the Consultant's officers, agents, and employees against any and all suits or claims that may be based upon the Consultant's work on behalf of the Client.

Part 11. No Third-Party Contracts

The Consultant shall have no authority to bind the Client in any way with third parties for the work defined within this Agreement.

Notices

All notices under this Agreement shall be mailed to the parties hereto at the following respective addresses:

SAMPLE CONTRACT

Great Company, LLC
c/o John Smith
1355 Queen Blvd. /4th Floor
Columbia, OH 43200
Phone: 555-555-4444
Fax: 555-555-4445

Towne Sports, Inc.
c/o Mary Jones
Address: 2001 Ashtown Rd.
Columbia, OH 43200
Phone: 555-555-5555
Fax: 555-555-5556

Each party must notify the other upon change of mailing address or other contact information with a written notice of such change.

Therefore, the parties have caused this agreement to be executed in duplicate this day and year first written above.

Great Company, LLC	Towne Sports, Inc.
Company	Client
______________________	______________________
Name	Name
______________________	______________________
Title	Title

Note: This contract is for illustrative purposes only and may no longer be appropriate for use in this or any other states. The reader should obtain legal council on the structure and language of any legal document prior to entering into any contract.

CHAPTER 3

WHERE TO FIND GRANTS & TYPES OF GRANTS

CASE STUDY: DIANNE HARRIS

"I hear you do grant writing. Do you know of some grants we can get?" This is a question I hear often. Although I have done a lot of grant writing in a particular field I do keep my antennae out to take note of ones that I think might be useful for my clients and their communities, and I try to send along that information when I find it.

Still, I think it would be impossible for any individual to have detailed knowledge of the thousands of foundations, the assistance they provide, and their particular requirements or restrictions. It is smart to network and ask everyone you know if anyone is aware of grant awards that are for programs similar to yours. But eventually, someone will have to expend the time and energy looking up, reading about, and making a determination whether or not each may be a possible source for you to approach.

The "Library Ladies" were a very effective organization in this respect. They had a major capital campaign to expand the community's library building. They located some catalogs of grant programs and began listing all foundations that funded building projects and those that funded library and educational related programs. They created a spreadsheet that included whether or not a letter of inquiry or letter of interest was required, application due dates, decision dates, range of award amounts, and average award amounts. In the last column they assigned members of their committee to conduct further explorations and those that should work on particular proposal. In all they had a list of more than 30 target foundations! They came to me for help with only five that they felt were too detailed for their level of expertise. With such a well-planned project, background work, and a coordinated team approach, it was easy to offer them a favorable rate for grant writing services.

— Dianne Harris

This chapter reveals resources for locating grants. It provides valuable links to directories and services, with thousands of listings for all types of assistance. But it also presents the differences between types of funders, such as governments, foundations, and research foundations, and the types of assistance given by each. An extensive, although not exhaustive, list of contact information can be found in the Appendix.

So where to start looking for grants? The most effective place to look depends on whether one is just starting out and is looking for some seed funding, whether there is an established organization with some earned startup funds, whether some programming already exists, or whether it is time to expand operations and offerings. Since hard work has achieved the current level of service, seeking out grants is a great way to leverage the work and funds already done to expand a program or begin another complementary one. Although planning for that new program must occur, it is natural to want to take a preliminary review of foundations to learn which ones support the type of activity you are considering. Make better use of your time and the effort invested by carefully reviewing available grants, their requirements, available amounts of assistance, and timing. Then develop a list of those that best fit your project. Limit your efforts to approaching those rather than a "shotgun" mass mailing to every foundation found.

To compare various grants it is helpful to create a spreadsheet or a chart that organizes the information about each potential funder, its focus, available funds, when each receives applications, and whether it prefers an initial contact through a letter of inquiry or other method prior to submission of a full proposal. Other requirements can also be listed in their own columns. A sample of such a chart, the Grant Sources Evaluation Tool, is included in the Appendix and on the companion CD-ROM.

DIRECTORIES

There are several directories of foundation support. Often some will be available in print at the local library. Increasingly, such directories and compendiums are available through Web sites. For example, **www.grantsalert.com** specializes in helping to locate education grants. Several others dedicated to education-related grants are listed later in this section under "Grants for Individuals." Even the American Dental Association (**www.ada.org**) has a foundation that provides material and network assistance to dentists that suffer losses due to natural disasters and may need help for their families or in re-establishing their practices.

Other sources of leads for grants are organizations formed for the purpose of networking in an area of specialty and for the purpose of increasing the skills and effectiveness of their members or of other local nonprofits. One of the best known is the Council on Foundations. Its Web site, **www.cof.org**, provides links to a number of grant source compendiums, information on grant writing, other resources for nonprofits, and seminars that might be useful to the grant seeker. Also well known is the Foundation Center, **www.fdncenter.org**. In addition to links to thousands of grant programs in the United States, it allows you to search its online database. The Foundation Center now compiles several targeted directories that are updated frequently. Some of its services are now by subscription, and if you are inclined to purchase lists of leads, it has one of the more reputable such services available by subscription.

Organizations created specifically to assist their members or the nonprofit world also periodically scan available grants and assistance, compile those that they think would be of interest to their members, and list contact information either on their Web sites or in their newsletters. These organizations increasingly have an online presence, whether through a Web site or e-mail newsletters. One such resource is **www.knowledgeplex.org**, which sends out periodic abstracts of news about affordable housing, whether it be setbacks in local legislation, related court cases, unique new initiatives, or uses for grant funds. Another site, **www.groundspring.org**, sponsored by the Ohio Governor's Office on Appalachia, provides e-mail newsletters with periodic abstracts on a wide range of grant opportunities. Its target audience works in economic development in rural areas, but the free service is available to anyone. With each of these there are links where you can further investigate opportunities that are applicable to each situation.

A clearinghouse of local direct assistance is found in many communities either through a First Link Catalog at the library or a Web site such as **www.firstlink.org**. First Link projects have a local phone number and office to direct questions to as well. The Northern California Community Foundation attempts to link the state's grant seekers with foundations and grant information (see **www.foundations.org**). Many other states and cities offer similar lists, specializing in locally or regionally available grants. An Internet search using keywords such as grants, foundations, and your community or state name should help you to hone in on these local resources.

The Catalog of Federal Domestic Assistance is perhaps the best known publication listing federal government programs and assistance. It also provides summaries of the legislation from which each form of assistance originates, along with program descriptions and eligibility. *The Catalog of Federal Domestic Assistance* can now be accessed on the Web at **www.cfda.gov**. Recently all federal agencies were mandated to publish information about all grant programs on a central site, **www.grants.gov**. Some may find this to be a more user-friendly site. Another closely related Web site is **www.gpoaccess.gov/nara/index.html**. Its features include the Federal Register and links to federal agency Web sites. Although it lists announcements of federal grant availability, it does not list geographically specific grants. Another useful clearinghouse is the Federal Citizen Information Center, sponsored by the General Services Administration (GSA). It can be accessed online at **www.pueblo.gsa.gov**, or by phone at 1-888-878-3256. The GSA's site provides access to toll-free numbers and contact information. Another excellent source for grant listings for nonprofit organizations is available through Michigan State University: **www.lib.msu.edu/harris23/grants**.

For those who are able to sell services as part of their revenue, a good source of potential projects is centralized government procurement programs. Many state and local governments operate Web sites with frequently updated listings, as well as instructions, hints, and downloadable forms. Larger cities may list their own projects, but states often provide information about local government opportunities, as well as state bids. It is even possible to register for e-mail notification of listings that conform to your specialized criteria. The Federal Business Opportunities Web site, **www.fedbizopps.gov**, lists opportunities for all federal agencies.

> **TIP:** *On the federal site it is also possible to view previous contract winners and look up their companies. Often these companies need independent subcontractors to perform portions of their project awards, especially for projects in which some of the work needs to be done away from the corporate office. A nonprofit, as well as any small company, could contact these larger companies directly to explore the possibility of working with them on a larger project.*

Another source of information, *Commerce Business Daily*, abstracts procurement and contract announcements that will be open for bidding.

- **www.grants.gov** — This is now the central clearinghouse of all federal grants. All federal agencies are now required to post their complete set of grant opportunities on **grants.gov**. It provides announcements when the grants are available, information about the application processes, descriptions of the programs' intent, due dates, contact information, and links to more information.

- **www.grantsalert.com** — This site claims to have a goal of simplifying the task of finding and winning grants for educational organizations. It has grant search capabilities, helpful hints, and samples. Beware some of the sponsors' claims, however.

PRE-PROPOSAL WORKSHOPS AND GRANT WRITING SEMINARS

Sometimes grant makers, especially government granting agencies, will hold training and information workshops for grant seekers that are specific to a particular grant program or a request for proposal. Although not set up to teach grant writing skills, these workshops can be valuable opportunities to learn in-depth information about complex or highly competitive grants. These pre-proposal meetings also provide additional opportunities to network with representatives of the granting agency, as well as others who may have applied for these funds in the past, and to learn from their experiences. Though there is often a requirement to register in advance and perhaps some travel costs involved, the pre-proposal workshop is normally free. Seminars that teach grant writing skills will often charge a fee.

Examples of the many organizations and grant programs that hold pre-proposal workshops include: The Assistance to Firefighters Grant (AFG), a competitive grant program accessed through the Federal Emergency Management Agency (FEMA) at **www.firegrantsupport.com**. These are two-hour workshops given at various locations throughout the country. They provide information about the grant program itself, the application process, and tips on drafting a successful narrative. These are free, and advance registration is not required. The Web site includes a downloadable basic presentation and other information if you are unable to attend the workshops. Another is the City of San Jose, California, Office of Cultural Affairs, which funds a number of grants for public art installation, neighborhood arts programs, special events such as parades, and operation grants for arts organizations. Some of its workshops include 90-minute presentations, but others are "drop in" events where staff is made available for individual question-and-answer sessions. These are also free, and the schedule is posted at **www.sanjoseculture.org**. The Grand Rapids, Michigan, affiliate of the Susan G. Komen for the Cure organization, which raises funds for breast cancer research, also provides free workshops for those interested in receiving its grants. Its workshops about its proposal solicitation and application process are also free, but reservations are recommended. It can be contacted at **www.komengr.org**.

One company that has created a business of grant writing training is the Washington, D.C.-based Grant Training Center, **www.granttrainingcenter.com**. Its seminars are often held at college and university locations and may be hosted by a local organization. You may find local advertising of a grant seminar that it is presenting. The basic seminars are three days in length, and fees are $595, not including travel, meals, and hotel costs. The Center also has provisions for memberships that include a newsletter, grant announcements, and a discount on one three-day seminar. Membership and attendance at a three-day seminar also has the benefit of one complimentary pre-submission proposal review each year.

Sometimes even the rating tool that will be used in a proposal evaluation phase is shared and explained. The rating tool might be a simple list of factors with scores assessed in each category, with the highest total scores being most likely to be funded. More complex rubrics might weight the scores of certain categories. The precise criteria by which the scores are achieved might be outlined, or the scoring might be more to the judgment of the individual members of the review team. The explanation of the rating tool might detail how the scoring done by several members of the review team gets compiled to a single score. Perhaps a simple average will be used, or perhaps totals of all categories. A highly simplified example of such a review tool follows. It does demonstrate how you can strategically work to overcome weaknesses when you understand the weight placed on some criteria. For example, you might not be able to do much about your community's demographics compared to another, but you can work extra hard on documenting your budget and implementation plan to maximize your points in those or, ideally, all other categories. Such explicit information can help the fine-tuning of a proposal to ensure you receive all the rating points your application is entitled to.

SIMPLE RANKING CRITERIA FORM			
Criteria	Rank 1-5	Weighting Factor	Subtotal
% Low Income Population	10% = 1 point 10-20% = 2 points 20-30% = 3 points 30-40% = 4 points >40% = 5 points	Point value x 5	10
Previous Grant Performance & Capacity of Staff	Excellent = 5 points Good = 4 points Fair = 2 points Poor or none = 0 points	Point value x 1	5
Statement of Need	Crisis = 5 points Urgent need = 4 point Limited extent but important need = 3 points Case for need not strong = 1 point	Point value x 5	15
Budget	Reasonable = 5 points Not well documented = 3 points Not at all supported = 0 points	Point value x 4	12
Implementation Plan	Highly feasible and well supported = 5 points Feasible and good use of resources = 4 points Average execution = 3 points Major features not explained = 1 point	Point value x 2	6

SIMPLE RANKING CRITERIA FORM			
Criteria	Rank 1-5	Weighting Factor	Subtotal
Match and Leverage of Resources	Greater than 1:1 cash match = 5 points Greater than 25% match in volunteer services = 4 points Blending with other grant funds greater than 0.5:1 = 3 points No match or in-kind = 0 points	Point value x 3	15
Grand Total			63 out of 90 possible

GUIDELINES

When some interesting funding opportunities have been identified, the next step is to contact the funder to obtain a copy of its grant guidelines, if they are available. The guidelines may state additional requirements for the grant program that may not appear elsewhere, such as how the reviewers prefer to see information organized, required documentation, and desired format of the material. There may be explicit information and somewhat minute details about the types of programs the funder wishes to support. Sometimes the guidelines do not reveal important information, so it is worthwhile to review multiple sources of information about a grant program prior to beginning the proposal writing process.

MATCHING THE PROGRAM TO THE FUNDER

Some grants are intended for very specific purposes. It is best to not waste time submitting proposals to the reviewing agency that obviously do not fit its criteria. Although it is true that sometimes a foundation might be flexible with its criteria or in response to a pet concern of one of its board members, do not assume this will be the case. Unless there has been an opportunity to become well acquainted with a board member, an invitation received to submit to the grantor, or otherwise solid information of the existence of flexible criteria revealed, it would be best to direct efforts toward those whose stated criteria are a close match with the proposed program.

WHAT KIND OF GRANT CAN I GET?

CASE STUDY: DIANNE HARRIS

Once I was working with a community to prepare a grant application for a housing improvement program for which the U.S. Department of Housing and Urban Development (HUD) was the main source of funds.

My community partners expressed a desire to structure the program in certain ways that did not conform to the stated program criteria. Although they had several convincing arguments about the wisdom of their program idea, I had to keep reiterating that their particular ideas were not eligible under HUD's criteria, which often are constrained by legislation. My co-worker explains the problem in this way, "It is as if HUD designed a suit, and maybe it fits you and maybe it doesn't. But if you want to use their (grant) money you will have to wear the HUD suit. You can let out a little of yourself here or there, but it will be the HUD suit." Consequently, it does not make sense to remake yourself or your project just to fit a particular funder's criteria if it causes you to lose your special focus or if it causes you to spend too many of your resources in meeting post-grant requirements. Keep looking for a grant that has the flexibility or focus that aligns with your special idea.

— **Dianne Harris**

This chapter also discusses eligibility requirements, the importance of forming partnerships, and the types of grants or other assistance available to an individual, not-for-profit, or governmental agency. We will look at whether you need to recruit outside assistance in researching or writing a grant, what to look for, and what to expect from the contracted relationship.

When researching your potential benefactors in the major catalogs, you will see notations about the types of programs, organizations, or projects the funder normally supports. Some will be restricted to very specific activities and sometimes geographic areas. Also pay attention to the types of organizations or individuals they support. They may fund only research projects, only residents of the community in which the benefactor is located, or only religious groups. Pay close attention to these guidelines before you invest time into preparing and sending off a proposal. Be strategic in compiling your list of potential sources. Find those that are most closely aligned with your project and mission.

Typical Grant Sources and Their Recipients

Individuals are most likely able to receive grants for research or perhaps creative arts projects. The most common type of support for an individual is through scholarships for advanced training, skills enhancement, or personal development. These may cover the cost of tuition or living expenses or sometimes both. Fellowships are awards for demonstrated accomplishment that often pay living expenses while the fellow pursues an academic research project, in some cases the completion of an advanced degree in a particular area of study. There are also a number of prizes and awards for past achievement in certain fields, for example, Pulitzer Prizes for literature, or the McArthur Genius-Innovation Awards. These types of awards are discussed later in this chapter.

Not-for-profit organizations and charities are the most frequent recipients of foundation support. Most foundations are created for the purpose of improving some element of their community, finding a cure for or promoting treatment of diseases, or improving some aspect of life for those who are less fortunate. Community foundations often also serve as clearinghouses for small private benevolent funds, providing asset management, disbursement, and administration services for those smaller funds. In those small funds, there can be a great deal of diversity as to the type of activity they wish to support. When researching a community foundation, you should look up and examine the smaller funds that they administer in addition to the community foundation's own funds. Corporate foundations are the vehicle through which major companies channel most of their major philanthropic endeavors, though they sometimes will contribute additional amounts to major special campaigns.

Governmental agencies and units of government are the most frequent recipients of grants from higher-level units of government, for example, the Community Development Block Grant (HUD) or Transportation Enhancement Grants (Department Of Transportation). Major research institutions or their researchers are the usual recipients of assistance through the National Institute of Health (NIH) or the U.S. Department of Defense and other federal agencies that benefit from special research projects.

GOVERNMENT GRANTS

The case study shown in Chapter 5 illustrates the usual chain of events for accessing federal grants, especially for home purchases and business development. Although many forms of assistance are available to home and business owners, there has been a lot of false advertising about government grants. These grants are never available to individuals or developers through application directly to the federal agency. Federal agencies such as Housing and Urban Development, the Department of Agriculture's Rural Development Agency, or the Small Business Administration (SBA) use locally based offices or partner agencies that distribute the grant monies in local communities. If interested in these funds for personal use, it is most effective to contact the local county- or city-based housing development departments, community action organizations (CAAs or CAOs), or small business development corporations (SBDC). Often this assistance is available in the form of low interest and sometimes forgivable loans (essentially a grant after the satisfaction of certain conditions). The exact way the funds will be deployed will vary from community to community according to the program designed by the locally based agency. More about the types of programs follows later in this chapter.

Other major federal grantors, such as the National Institute of Health or the National Endowment for the Arts (NEA), provide grants that are accessed for major, basic research projects and provide support for a period of time to recognized artists to produce major artworks. These are highly specialized and highly competitive, mostly available only to those who have already demonstrated a significant level of accomplishment or potential.

Grants from the Department of Transportation (DOT) and the Environmental Protection Agency (EPA) are most of the time available only to local governments for major infrastructure projects. Many states have grants for road and bridge work, as well as water and waste water projects for local governments to access. Smaller communities are often aware that assistance may be available for these purposes. It is often required that a portion of the project be paid for by locally raised money, which is referred to as the local "match." For example, a 50 percent match requirement means that the government grant will pay for half of the total allowable project costs. Matching requirements are sometimes viewed by the funding source as "leveraged" funds toward accomplishing their purposes in providing grants. The setting aside of local funds to provide matches for such projects can sometimes be a difficult endeavor. Those in the community that are not fully aware of these requirements may see the funds that are being held for later use as "excess" available for any competing project. Politicians might see these savings as "excess" that justifies the reduction of taxes for the citizens, especially in an election year. Therefore, even at the government level, it is important to communicate to the residents the community's level of need for a variety of capital projects, the associated costs, needed match reserves, the degree of priority, and the plan for how such improvements will be fully financed.

GRANTS FOR INDIVIDUALS

In this section you will find descriptions and some special sources of the major categories of grants for individuals, including:

- Grants and residencies for artists
- Grants for teachers
- Grants for home buyers or home repairs
- Small business owners
- Special awards to volunteers
- Special awards for exceptional achievement
- Contests
- Scholarships, fellowships, and other education-related grants

Grants and Residencies for Artists

Grants for artists may provide funds for expenses such as small living stipends while a work of art is being completed, travel expenses associated with research or reaching an audience, expenses of materials, or a stipend to defray the cost of preparing a prototype or developing a concept proposal for a potential client. Often prizes can be earned for works or art that have already been produced.

Residencies may provide a dwelling and living stipend while researching an academic project or producing a work of art. These sometimes require a limited amount of interaction with aspiring artists, a gallery show, performances, or lectures. Far from being "work," these are opportunities to reach out to an audience, to increase your professional recognition, to develop a customer base, and to "give back" to one's craft, while still providing significant free time to pursue your art.

An example of a residency is awarded by The Thurber House in Columbus, Ohio at the restored historic home of writer and humorist James Thurber. The literary nonprofit that oversees the building supports many literature-based activities for the community. One is the Writer-in-Residency Program in Children's Literature. The residency offers an emerging writer of literature for middle grade students a free, one-month summer retreat in a furnished apartment in The Thurber House, and it comes with a cash stipend as well. The writer is invited to teach writing seminars to children for only ten hours each week and has time to work on his or her own writing projects as well.

Literary prizes that recognize completed works are common, and The Thurber House also presents several annual cash prizes to support writers in the amount of $5,000 each. One is the Thurber Prize for American Humor. For this, the writer must be nominated by a publisher or agent. Information about applications can be found at **www.thurberhouse.org**. Others are the Columbus Literary Awards, which recognize three central Ohio writers, one each in the category of fiction, nonfiction, and poetry.

Writers as well as other professionals have several opportunities each year to gather with others at conferences. The conference fees, travel, hotel, and meals can get quite expensive. Though not advertised, it is possible to approach the organization for a fee waiver, especially where there is financial hardship. This request should be done well in advance, in writing, and follow a format similar to a grant letter of inquiry. Students of a future profession can avail themselves of reduced or free fees in a similar manner. Some organizations publish the student discount in the conference registration materials.

Sources of Arts Grants

The National Endowment for the Arts, **www.NEA.gov**, is an independent federal agency that provides major support for a wide spectrum of arts in

America. Its focus is largely on the area of important innovative techniques and the preservation of the skills important to nationally significant art and craft traditions. Although the NEA mostly supports arts organizations, it does provide individual grants such as Literature Fellowships, NEA Jazz Masters Fellowships, and NEA National Heritage Fellowships in the Folk and Traditional Arts.

In addition to national and statewide arts organizations, the artistic grant seeker may find that his or her town or region has one or more small groups dedicated to support of the various arts: literary, theatrical, musical, performance, visual, sculptural, and even for interior, landscape, or architectural design. Some examples of locally based artist grants and residencies follow. A great side benefit of a residency is the opportunity to travel and even live in a community for a short time.

- **www.arts.state.tn.us** — The Tennessee Touring Arts Program provides grants of $350 to $4,000 to Tennessee artists to take their work into under-served communities across the state.

- **www.palmbeachculture.com** — The Palm Beach County Cultural Council funds artist-in-residency programs, consisting of up to $30,000 for a three- to nine-month residency in the county.

- **http://artscouncil.ky.gov** — The Individual Artist Professional Development Program was created to assist Kentucky artists with professional development through workshops, conferences, classes, or participation in a performance or exhibition. Grants are for up to 50 percent of total project costs, to a maximum of $500.

- **www.massculturalcouncil.org** — The Massachusetts Cultural Council gives grants of between $5,000 and $7,500 to Massachusetts artists to enable them to have time to hone their abilities.

Grants for Teachers

The world of foundations has recognized the field of teaching in particular as an area where individuals deserve grants to help provide better in-classroom instruction. The profession of teaching is known for relatively low pay scales compared to the education, responsibility, and level of experience that teachers need to be certified. In spite of this, many teachers purchase additional books, tools, and classroom supplies from their own income. Some states require teachers to invest in continuing education to maintain their accreditation, which is another expense. Although the Internal Revenue Service now allows educators a special deduction from their taxable income for the cost of additional class supplies, this deduction is limited to $250, all receipts must be kept, and a deduction from income does not recoup the full cost of the supplies purchased.

The most common types of grants for teachers cover expenses such as:

- Books
- Supplies
- Conference fees
- Travel expenses to conferences
- Continuing education tuition

Other common types of cash awards for teachers include:

- Awards for accomplishments in special categories of instruction
- Awards for development of a curriculum that incorporates special fields of study

Sources of Grants and Grant Information for Teachers

Educators have become engaged in networking, sharing information, and creating resources for their fellow educators to adapt and use. A sampling of such resources follows:

- **www.agclassroom.org** — The U.S. Department of Agriculture, Agriculture in the Classroom Program gives small grants for classroom excellence in incorporating the importance of agriculture into classroom instruction and, with local soil and water conservation districts, grants to pay expenses for attending conferences.

- **www.schoolgrants.org** — SchoolGrants, a private consulting company, provides assistance with finding and obtaining grants, specifically for teachers. It also has "Going for the Gold" grant workshops for educators and fee-based grant writing services.

- **www.eschoolnews.com** — See this Web site for education news, developments, resources, and especially the "Grants and Funding" area for references to other grant programs.

- **www.techlearning.com** — The Technology and Learning Web site does not sponsor grants itself, but it provides a compendium of grants of special interest to educators that is not restricted to technology-related programs. Look under "Funding" in the "Hot Topics" corner of the site. It also provides grant writing tips and other fund-raising ideas.

- **www.OCE-OCS.org** — The Office of Catholic Education has resources, including funding for educational programs in Catholic-sponsored schools.

- **www.ohiomsa.org** — The Ohio Middle School Association provides small grants and the opportunity to present at a conference and to produce an article to be published in the OMSA Journal. It recognizes replicable interdisciplinary educational units.

- **www.ed.gov/fund** — The U.S. Department of Education gives grants and research funding to states, school districts, and colleges for improving instruction, research, and special program needs.

Though not an individual grant, an individual teacher might spearhead a district grant application that benefits more than his or her own classroom.

- **www.neh.gov** — The National Endowment for the Humanities has grants for curriculum development and for classroom materials to promote excellence in education in the humanities.

- **www.collegeboard.com/counselors/teachers** — CollegeBoard.com's "Bob Costas Grants for the Teaching of Writing" gives $3,000 awards for teachers using innovative ways to inspire good writing by their students.

- **www.hp.com/go/hpteach** — Hewlett-Packard Company provides millions in grants for wireless technology, cash, and professional development to schools and classrooms across the country.

- **www.tolerance.org** — Tolerance.org is a project of the Southern Poverty Law Center and grants funds for developing and launching anti-bias curricula and projects in the classrooms and throughout a community, called "Teaching Tolerance Grants Program."

- **www.crlt.umich.edu** — The University of Michigan, Center for Research on Learning and Teaching has several grants to promote better teaching skills for instructors working at the Ann Arbor Campus of University of Michigan.

- **www.mcg.edu** — The Medical College of Georgia gives grants to promote the use of cutting-edge technology in medical school instruction.

- **www.twc.org**—The Teachers and Writers Collaborative Fellowships for early career writers includes a $10,000 stipend, office space, equipment, and a mentor in New York City.

- **www.pga.com** — Jack Nicholas/Professional Golf Association's First Tee Program Grants gives $5,000 grants to First Tee Programs to encourage teaching young people of all backgrounds, races, and genders the game of golf and values such as good sportsmanship.

Free Lesson Plans

Teachers can often find free help with their lesson planning functions, which can greatly reduce their work time out of the classroom. Sources of pre-developed lesson plans include:

- **www.irs.gov**, keywords, "teacher expense deductions" — The IRS has developed a set of lesson plans about our tax system and completing tax forms. These may be used in courses such as history, social studies, civics/government, economics, and technology and are designed to reinforce state and national standards in education.

- **www.agclassroom.org** — The USDA has developed a set of lesson plans called "Growing a Nation" about the role of agriculture in the history of the United States and a set about natural resources and agriculture for science classes.

Grants and Help with Buying, Repairing or Renting a Home

Two major grant programs to improve housing and access to good quality housing are the HOME Investment Partnerships and Community Development Block Grants. They are passed to the consumer through the local or county development department. These funds can be used for grants or very low interest loans a variety of purposes:

- Down payments to buy a home

- Funds to pay for home repairs

- Emergency rent payments

- Emergency mortgage payments
- Subsidized rent payments
- Reduce the purchase price of a home
- Funds to pay for handicap-accessible modifications to a home
- Funds to build rental properties
- Funds to renovate rental properties

Admittedly, low interest loans are of course funds that do require repayment, but the low interest and sometimes forgivable terms provided by these programs are a significantly better "deal" than any banking institution will offer you. As such, the dollars saved by going this route should be regarded as in effect "free."

If you live in a very rural area, similar programs are available through the U.S. Department of Agriculture, Rural Development agency. Information can be found online at **www.rurdev.usda.gov** or through your county development department.

State Help with Buying a Home or Lowering Rental Costs

State Housing Finance Agencies have a variety of programs available for similar purposes and which vary somewhat according to each state. The chief program that is available to all is authorized by the U.S. Tax Code and is called the Low Income Housing Tax Credit. Examples of these programs include:

- Free funds for down payments to buy a home
- Free funds for closing costs when buying a house
- Free funds to lower the interest rate of buying a house

- Tax credits for building or renovating affordable houses or apartments
- Low interest loans for building or renovating affordable houses or apartments

Renovating Historic Homes

Federal tax credits are available for restoration of income-producing historic properties. Although a long process, the amount of assistance is significant. Increasingly, individual states and some cities are authorizing tax credits or other incentives for homeowners that wish to restore a historic property. Although tax credits do not provide funds up front, they are dollar-for-dollar reductions of a tax bill and are sometimes spread over several years. Historic homes are also eligible for the generic repair grants and the energy efficiency programs listed here.

Energy Efficiency Home Improvements

Currently, the U.S. Tax Code allows for credits off individuals' tax bills if they have made energy savings improvements to their homes. Improvements that are paid for include energy-efficient air conditioning and heating units, new energy-efficient windows, installation of solar panels, and installation of insulation. These tax credits are in addition to the benefit of the lower utility cost that will be obtained from the new fixtures. These credits are subject to being eliminated but have been effective in promoting fuel savings, so watch for updates to tax instructions each year for changes to the program.

Help with Utility Bills and Energy Costs

The U.S. Department of Health and Human Services, Administration for Children and Families, **www.liheap.ncat.org**, provides grant funds to assist with utility costs on an ongoing and also on an emergency basis. These funds are distributed to the consumer through local sponsors, such as local development departments, Community Action Agencies, and Area Agencies on Aging. Other state and local funds are often combined with the federal funds to increase the number of people who can be served. Application for these funds is much simpler than for other grant applications; you need only complete a short information package including documentation of your residency, income, and utility costs. Processing time for these grants can sometimes be longer than you want, so it is important to contact the agency to get on its list early in the heating/cooling season, before you fall behind on payments.

- PIPP — Percentage Income Payment Plan
- HEAP — Home Energy Assistance Program
- EHEAP — Emergency Energy Assistance Program
- HWAP — Home Weatherization Assistance Program

Business Owners

Small Business Startups

Microbusiness development grant programs are administered in a variety of ways in various locations and by various agencies. Federal Community Development Block Grants may be used for this purpose, and other locally generated funds may be available. Check with your county or local department of economic development to see if it or a local agency it knows of administers microbusiness programs. These programs, in most cases, are for the startup or expansion of a business with very few employees other than the owner. The amount of funds will vary but may be used for entrepreneurial training, purchase of inventory, equipment, merchandising displays, signs, repairs, and improvements to the interior of a business. Applications for these funds are simple and will resemble a consumer loan application, asking for a lot of information about the state of the business or the readiness to launch the business. They do not require a lot of "creative" writing, just a clear presentation of the facts.

Once considered a source of grant funds, in recent years, the U.S. Small Business Administration has not received funding to make grants to individuals or small businesses. Still SBA has developed a number of programs to provide other assistance to businesses that are small in size, the definition of which varies according to industry. A manufacturing business of less than 500 employees, a wholesale company of less than 100 employees, or an agricultural business of less than $0.75 million in revenue per year are all considered "small" by the SBA. SBA programs include:

- Small Business Innovations Research (SBIR)
- Small Business Investment Companies (SBIC)
- Small Business Technology Transfer (SBTT)
- Small Disadvantaged Business (SDB)
- Service Corps Of Retired Executives (SCORE)
- Women In Business (WIB)
- HUB Zone Empowerment Contracting (HUB)
- ProNet

SBA grants are given only to local-level SBICs and SBIRs to conduct their various loan programs, including the SBTT, SDB, and WB. These programs are intended to provide access to financing, not grants. The agency does provide a large amount of free support given directly to individuals or their businesses in the form of advice, free training, and use of resource and reference material. A great deal is available from its Web site, **www.**

sba.gov, and also from your local SCORE office. HUB and ProNet are resources to help connect the small business with government procurement opportunities or subcontracting opportunities with larger government contractors.

Women- and Minority-Owned Businesses

To fill in the gap left of grant funding for businesses and foundations, local initiatives that recognize the value of stimulating the growth of small businesses have evolved. One example is **www.womensinitiative.org**, a San Francisco group that provides $9,000 for the deposit and first month lease costs (First Time Lease Holder Grants) for storefronts for women-owned startups in San Francisco neighborhoods.

In addition to the First Time Lease Holder Grants, this group offers pre-startup loans, startup loans, and operating capital loans for women-owned small businesses that have trouble getting traditional financing.

Assistance to Existing Small Businesses

The Entrepreneur Center of San Jose, a model of small business support, provides a resource center with free use of computers and other office equipment, research tools, library, and videos for business training and assistance with business planning. The dollar value of such assistance depends on how much use each business owner makes of the available services.

Business Incubators

The EnterPrize Business Plan Competition, a project of the Pittsburg Technology Council, **www.pghtech.org**, is open to residents and students in southwestern Pennsylvania. This clever project awards cash prizes to companies, in both the new startup and existing business categories, who develop the best business plans after having gone through a process of meeting with experienced advisors over a period of about six months. Even if the business does not win an award, it has received free business planning advice while going through the process.

Specifically for Land Owners and Farmers

The Private Stewardship Grants Program, U.S. Fish and Wildlife Service, **www.fws.gov**, grants to individual property owners or partnerships of organizations and property owners to provide incentive to plan and protect habitat of threatened or endangered species found on the land.

Economic Development Funds for Larger Businesses

Communities seldom offer outright grants to a larger business but are creative in using grant funds to "leverage" other investments, that is, to provide significant economic incentives or discounts to make growth of a business to be more feasible. Communities may use their Federal Community Development Block Grants and other state and locally generated funds to stimulate business investments that will create jobs and subsequent tax revenues for the community. The Federal Department of Commerce's Economic Development Administration also provides grants to communities specifically for these uses.

These programs may take many forms. A community may use its grant funds to build roads, install utilities, or increase water treatment capacities to make it more feasible for an industry to build in a certain location. This saves the developer or business owner those costs when building or expanding a new facility. A funder may use its grant money and other funds to provide very low interest loans to the business for the acquisition of major machinery.

Some communities will even refund to an employer a portion of local income tax generated by the employees of a major corporation, provided the total new tax from that employer reaches a minimum level.

All these techniques save the business significant amounts of money, albeit sometimes at a future date, which amounts to "free" money. Communities wishing to access Community Development Block Grants or Economic Development Administration Grants should review the requirements established by the respective federal agencies, Housing and Urban Development and the Department of Commerce. Businesses wishing to access these funds are advised to contact local, county, and state departments of development in their area to inquire about these programs. The application process can be quite long, but the community will do most of the grant application for you as long as you provide to them all the information and documentation possible, as soon as possible, when the business starts consideration of an expansion or relocation decision.

Special Awards to Volunteers

Volunteers are active for their causes because they want to give back to their communities or serve a higher calling. Financial reward is not the motivation for what they do. Even so, foundations and programs have been created to recognize volunteers' exceptional service and often to help raise awareness for the causes the volunteers support.

Sometimes, as in the case of the International Association of Chiefs of Police, an organization itself can be recognized for success in nurturing a volunteer force that augments the work of a paid professional agency in a community.

Types of Awards for Volunteerism

Awards programs for volunteers may involve simply a ceremony and a meal, a photo in a local paper, certificates, plaques, or medallions. Many organizations at least plan an annual luncheon or dinner to thank their volunteers. However, some supporters provide a little more in the way of cash awards, paid attendance at a conference or other event, gift certificates, presents, or scholarships for the chosen volunteer. These awards are given to teens and children involved in volunteerism. Some sponsors offer significant donations to the cause supported by the award winner. This allows the volunteer to multiply the benefit gained as a result of his or her efforts.

The range of awards types made for volunteerism include a few widely known programs. For example, the Jefferson Awards for Public Service are sponsored by media outlets, and awards are given at the local and national levels. The award consists of a specially designed medal and media publicity for the cause of the recipient. The National Make a Difference Day, started by *USA Weekend* magazine, celebrates volunteerism throughout local communities. Recipients of local awards are eligible for consideration for the national awards. Receiving a national award can win a $10,000 donation to the recipient's chosen charity. Prudential Financial awards scholarships at the level of $1,000 and $5,000 to chosen high school students that have volunteered a significant amount of time to a cause. Prudential also donates another $5,000 to the chosen cause of the national winner.

Applying for Volunteer Recognition

In contrast to grants and contests, most volunteer recognition programs are not applied for directly by the volunteer, but rather the volunteer is nominated by someone who acknowledges the significance of the group's efforts. Instructions for making the nominations can be obtained through grant guidelines, company or foundation Web sites, or by writing or calling the sponsoring organization.

Where to Look for Available Awards for Volunteers

Neither do there seem to be the same types of catalog compilations of information about volunteer awards as can be found for other types of grants and scholarships. Some contacts are listed here, but if you are interested in these awards, it pays to watch and make note when newspapers and other publications make announcements of such honors being bestowed.

- **www.prudential.com** — Information about student awards and scholarships
- **www.aips.org** — Information about The Jefferson Awards national organization
- **www.theiacp.org** — Police departments with volunteer programs
- **www.usaweekend.com/diffday** — Make a Difference Day project information
- **www.Kohlscorporation.com** — Information about student awards, scholarships, and other foundation programs

Special Awards for Exceptional Achievement

Some very prestigious grants are given out as recognition for outstanding achievement or demonstrated potential for innovation. A few examples are highlighted in this section. The MacArthur Fellows and the Nobel Laureates are examples of unrestricted grants to individuals, but one cannot make a normal application for them.

MacArthur Fellows Awards

One of the most significant awards that is truly "no strings attached" is the MacArthur Fellows Program, an award of $500,000 in support of an individual, not a program. This is not a grant that recognizes a specific achievement, but the individual's demonstrated talent, potential, and dedication to a creative pursuit. Past recipients have engaged in such diverse pursuits as writing, entrepreneurialism, and amateur scientific study. In 2006 the 25 recipients included David Carroll, a conservationist, author, and illustrator with expertise in wetland ecology, and Regina Carter, a jazz violinist with classical training. MacArthur Fellows can receive the award only through nomination by experts. See **www.Macfound.org** for more information on the Fellows awards and for how to apply for other programs sponsored by the John D. and Catherine T. MacArthur Foundation.

Nobel Prizes

The Nobel Foundation was established by Dr. Alfred Nobel in his will. By now, more than 20 organizations and 777 individuals have received the Nobel Prize in one of five categories: physics, chemistry, medicine, peace, and literature. These awards can be achieved only if nominated, and the Nobel Committees solicit the nominations from members of academies, governmental leaders, university professors, and even past Nobel Laureates (prize winners). The prize varies with the value of the interest generated by the endowment, which is divided equally by the five prize winners. In 2007 that was estimated to be one-fifth of 10,000,000 Swedish Kronas. The Nobel Prize also has no restrictions on its use. Albert Einstein, recipient of the award for physics, agreed in his divorce settlement to give the prize money to his first wife if he would ever win it (and he did honor that agreement). See **www.nobelprize.org** for more information about the prize and the foundation and even fun science exercises.

Innovations Awards

Even governmental agencies and their private-sector partners can receive awards for exceptional achievement, for example, the Innovations in American Government Awards, which are given by the ASH Institute for Democratic Governance and Innovation in the John F. Kennedy School of Government at Harvard University. For more information about this online application, visit **www.innovationsaward.harvard.edu**. These awards look for several criteria demonstrating achievement and innovation, including: novelty of the program, effectiveness in meeting objectives, significance in addressing an important problem in society, and transferability potential to other communities. The grant rewards programs that have been in operation for one year or longer. Eligible applicants are restricted to any unit of government or other entities that involved significant government involvement and oversight in the program. Those that meet these high standards are eligible for one of seven $100,000 grants to develop dissemination activities for the program in cooperation with the Innovations staff.

Contests

A contest is a very special type of award that often does not involve a standard grant application. Contest prizes are funded through sponsor donations and/or entry fees. An entry may be as simple as submitting evidence of skill or expertise, a work of art, literature, or other creative work. The entry may require a written narrative that explains the work, its objectives, its methodology, and its significance, similar to the way that a grant-funded program would be presented, as described in this book.

Contest awards may include cash prizes, publicity through publication or a gallery showing, and other non-cash prizes. Although a work product may be needed to be submitted with the entry, it is expected that one would submit work that has already been produced. Thus the contestant is able to receive an additional benefit and recognition for the effort of making the entry as prescribed in the contest guidelines.

Because of the high degree of expense required for participation in "scholarship contests," previously called "beauty pageants," for young ladies, it does not appear that the value of various prizes awarded really produces a net benefit for the contestants and so amounts to a purely "recreational" activity. Expenses include designer dresses and costumes, lessons to develop a "talent," fitness training, hair styling, cosmetics, coaching, and travel. Although, one could argue that when successful, the prizes do somewhat offset the costs of participation in the activity.

Scholarships, Fellowships, and Other Education Grants

The student about to embark on advancing his or her education beyond the high school level is going to be the primary recipient of scholarships and education-related grants. Although most may be limited to the high school or college student for eligibility, there are some that are intended for the "adult learner," that is to say, someone who has been out of school for more than a year and is now inspired to pursue advanced education or specific occupational training. There are awards that are available to younger students to cover the costs of private or special-purpose schools or simply meant to be held until the youngster is ready to pursue college.

Some grantors refer to these types of awards as "scholarships;" others call them "tuition assistance," "gifts," or other nomenclature. If the money does not have to be paid back, it works like a grant. For the rest of this section, the whole class of awards meant to help pay for education, whether tuition, room and board, books and supplies, or miscellaneous expenses will, for simplicity's sake, be referred to as scholarships.

Scholarships are one category of grants that do not follow the usual grant application format. Each scholarship sponsor will have its own method and requirements for application. The ones presented here are some of the common ones, but this list is by no means exhaustive.

Primary and Secondary Education Vouchers

Students who have attended schools that have not attained required improvements as evaluated by the National No Child Left Behind Act are eligible for education vouchers. These pay some or all the cost of tuition to a private school, or even an online school, that has a better record of educating its students. In areas where a choice of private schools is not available, the public school must provide free "supplemental education" such as tutoring or after-school programs. The details of the program, which schools are eligible, and the amount of the voucher are different in each state.

Many private schools also have endowments to provide free tuition for students that meet certain criteria. For example, a parochial school might make free or reduced tuition available to members of the sponsoring congregation. The National Catholic Education Association recommends that families contact their local arch/diocesan offices for information about financial aid available in their local Catholic schools.

High School and College Students

The number of scholarships available to high school and college students are much more varied than what one might imagine. Scholarships are not limited to students with stellar academic or athletic performance. More information about this will follow. Also, scholarships vary in whether they pay the award directly to the college for your tuition and housing payment, or whether the funds will be paid directly to the student for other expenses.

A student will be fortunate to have a high school counselor who provides information and resources about scholarships, especially ones that are limited to your region. Parents or guardians should be willing to assist the student in searching for scholarships and organizing the application process. Although scholarships of significant amounts are available, like the coveted "free ride," or "full scholarship," many more are for more modest amounts, often at least $500. It is entirely allowable to secure several smaller awards to substantially finance a college education. When layering awards, try to obtain some that are payable directly to the student for use for books, supplies and miscellaneous, or off-campus living expenses, if that will be the student's housing arrangement.

Students should complete an application form at **www.fafsa.ed.gov**, which is the most widely used application by colleges and universities to evaluate the amount and types of financial aid they can offer.

Just like other forms of grants, it may be necessary to reapply each year of your college career, or to replace single-year scholarships with new ones as you advance through college.

Some scholarships are available to high school students only, in preparation for their college years. Some are even restricted to high school seniors. Others will be available only to students that are actively enrolled in college or accepted to start in the next academic year. Others will be available to high school and college students.

Therefore, if you are successful in obtaining a scholarship targeted toward high school seniors only, it will be necessary to apply to a different scholarship in subsequent years that is available to college students. Even if you have received an award that continues to be available to both high school and college students, the award is most likely to be given out over a single year and will require a repeat application for the following year.

Looking for Scholarships

Scholarships are not as likely to be found in the foundation directories and directories of grants targeted toward nonprofit groups. Fortunately, there are directories of scholarships and many searchable Internet sites for scholarships and internships. FastWeb (**www.fastweb.com**) allows the user to input a profile and search its database for eligible scholarships. One can even sign up for e-mail alerts when new scholarships become available, including the new funding round for known scholarships. It provides basic information such as the title of the scholarship program, application deadline, and the amount available. It has a number of other useful functions related to planning for and paying for college. One does have to navigate through a few popup ads, but the service is entirely free to the student.

Scholarships can be found for just about every academic specialty, future occupation, volunteer interest, religious affiliation, extracurricular activity, and sport that can be imagined. Not all will be available at every school. Therefore it is a good tactic to research potential colleges based on the types of scholarships and aid they make available. One doesn't necessarily have to be in the top of his or her class to receive these. It is therefore important to complete in detail the college application sections about extracurricular activities, volunteerism, and interests. One should also be a little flexible about where he or she will attend school and what to study. When I was in high school, our language teacher informed us that there was a college that would give a full scholarship to anyone who would commit to a major with four years of study of the ancient Greek language at the school. We all rolled our eyes at the prospect, not realizing we could also still pursue our other interests. Later, when I labored for five years repaying undergraduate loans, I understood what a dope I had been for not looking into it. Though I no longer remember what this program was, an Internet search using search terms such as "scholarships ancient Greek" will turn up several scholarships for the study of Greek and other ancient languages.

The National Catholic Education Association, **www.ncea.org**, provides a number of grants for individuals and schools for education research and teacher training in Catholic education.

Search the Colleges' Federal Programs

The first place to look for scholarships and tuition payments is with the college or educational institution itself. Its application forms may have a question about whether the student will be seeking scholarships. The college itself will provide the access to scholarships that have been established exclusively for students attending that school. These may be tied to academic performance, academic major field of study, talent in a sport, or artistic talent and are often based on demonstrated financial need. Nearly all colleges use the Free Application for Federal Student Aid (FAFSA) **www.fafsa.ed.gov**, as the basis for need-based scholarships, not only for those available only through the school, but also the federal scholarships programs: the Federal Pell Grant (Pell), the Federal Academic Competitiveness Grant (ACG), and the National SMART Grant (Science and Mathematics Access to Retain Talent).

A Note About Internships

Internships are on-the-job learning experiences for future professionals. Some internships do not even come with pay. True, at first this may not sound like a grant, or even a good deal, but internships are worth a brief mention. To be awarded an internship is a form of a gift that will have long-term impact on your bottom line. Getting an internship is competitive, and not everyone will have this opportunity.

Some careers are extremely difficult to break into and require some amount of relevant work history. Therefore, first of all, internships present a wonderful opportunity to gain valuable work experience. Second, a well-placed internship can provide you with contacts that are even more valuable to your future, that is, the chance to become acquainted with (and impress) decision-makers and leaders in the field. Third, in many fields, interns are trained and directly recruited by the companies they have interned with, so that the internship is the only track for a job placement with some companies.

But, on the more rewarding side, some college internships not only come with modest pay, but also with "fee or tuition waivers." That means some or all the tuition is waived, or not paid back, which is the part that works like a grant. So, one might be able to gain experience, contacts, job recruitment, maybe a small salary, and free tuition. That's a lot of return for a small amount of work. Many engineering programs offer internships or other co-op arrangements. I was able to return to college full time at Ohio State University and gain my master's degree because of the fee and tuition waiver associated with my internship. By living frugally on the pay I received for 20 hours a week, and with the tuition waiver (grant), I was able to complete my degree in the usual two years, without taking out a student loan. In addition I was able to meet many of our city's leaders and obtain an introduction to my future employer. It's hard to even quantify that type of benefit. When I applied for admission, I simply needed to inform the advisor that I was interested in receiving financial aid, and I was automatically put in contact with the chair of the internship program. The individual agencies interviewed several prospective interns referred to their agencies through the graduate program, and eventually everyone got matched up.

Examples of Student Fellowships

The Harry Frank Guggenheim Foundation (HFG) provides fellowships for advanced study in the fields of the natural and social sciences and the humanities which examine the issues of violence, aggression, and dominance. The foundation supports postdoctoral research and dissertation fellowships, awards of $15,000 to individuals who will complete the writing of their dissertation that year.

The Fulbright Scholars Program is administered by the Council for International Exchange of Scholars (CIES) on behalf of the U.S. Department of State, Bureau of Educational and Cultural Affairs. There are several Fulbright Scholars grants, the best known being the program that allows 800 U.S. faculty and professionals to travel abroad each year to speak and conduct their research in a number of fields.

RESEARCH GRANTS

Some foundations exist only to raise funds for research and education. These are the usual types of grants given by the NIH. For example, it is of no use to contact PanCan (the Pancreatic Cancer Action Network) to request funds to take individuals affected by pancreatic cancer to Disney World. Although this might be a very noble project, PanCan was created expressly to generate research funding to find a cure for this disease and to provide a forum for the exchange of information on treatment and research results for the ultimate benefit of patients and their families facing treatment decisions. A physician engaged in pancreatic cancer research may find that PanCan may be a very good resource of funding for a research program.

COMMUNITY FOUNDATIONS

Community foundations are formed to benefit their local community or region exclusively. These foundations fund a variety of charitable, educational, and sometimes even government projects. They receive their funds from major donors in the community. Community foundations can serve as a central clearinghouse for other small, locally active foundations' grants and scholarships. In addition, the community foundation may generate income from the provision of administrative services for smaller private foundations or charities that engage in their own fund-raising or have dedicated donors. These may be too small to efficiently handle the many accounting, reporting, and grant awards processes and investments in endowments and other activities required of a nonprofit by state and federal law. For projects that have a particularly local interest, it is well worth contacting the community foundation, not only for its own programs, but also for referrals to smaller local grantors.

DONATIONS AND CONTRIBUTIONS

Grant support for building projects, such as "bricks and mortar" projects or for endowments, is harder to locate than for services and programs. It is easier to find grants for operations costs, research, education, or social service projects. Agencies wishing to construct or renovate facilities for their use must rely on capital campaigns to obtain outright donations, and very large projects, like new hospital wings, depend on major support from wealthy philanthropists or local corporations. Endowments are funded in similar ways to create a fund that can be used for long-term recurring operations costs, including utilities, insurance, maintenance, or other purposes. However, those sponsoring the creation of endowments often organize fund-raising events, dinners, galas, golf outings, and the like for the bulk of their funds. It is important to have a comprehensive fund-raising strategy that develops several sources of funds, some of which will be specific for only one of an organization's several purposes.

Sometimes support for such activities will be constructed as "challenge" grants. The challenge grant operates in a manner similar to the matching requirement in some grants. In the challenge grant or donation, the donor makes a promise of a donation (or grant) but will deliver it only if others will provide additional donations to that project, according to some stated proportion. The challenge grant is meant to inspire others in the community to make a similar commitment to the cause within a given time. It can also be used to inspire an organization to become more effective at other fund-raising endeavors. If the challenge is not met, the first pledge might also be lost.

HISTORIC PRESERVATION

One area in which building projects are expressly supported is the field of preservation of historic properties. In recent years, communities and organizations have become more aware of the importance of such structures to community image and community life and, as a result, have become active in restoring these historic structures. Neglected for years, these properties often need extensive and expensive repairs. If this is an area of interest, the following sources may be helpful. One example of grant funding for restoring historic buildings is the "Save America's Treasures" grant; information can be found at **www.cr.nps.gov/hps/treasures**. Other sources include the Getty Grants, **www.getty.edu/grants/conservation/arch_planning.html**, the National Trust for Historic Preservation Grants to Nonprofits and Governments, **www.nationaltrust.org/funding**, and the National Center for Preservation, Technology and Training Grants, **www.ncptt.nps.gov**. It is also worth exploring for funding from the state's historic preservation office and perhaps the city or county. There may be special programs for preserving historic structures or sites in the community. Pennsylvania and Indiana are particularly active in fostering historic preservation efforts. An emerging tool is that of donation of façade easements to a preservation organization. These might be "cashless" donations, but they might significantly assist the preservationists in keeping the community historic fabric intact. The owner gains a tax benefit for the value of the donation and retains control of the structure's interior. The community gets a guarantee that the street "face" of the building will be maintained in its familiar historic character without the expense of purchasing and maintaining the building.

More About Grants for Individuals

As stated earlier, individuals interested in assistance with securing housing or housing funds should contact their local department of development, community action organization, Metropolitan Housing Authority, State Housing Development Finance Agency, local not-for-profit housing development corporations, and even local bankers to determine what types of housing programs are operating locally and whether or not they qualify. Most direct housing assistance is in the form of very low or zero-rate interest or sweat-equity programs. Rarely, there may be small grants available for critical repair work. Individuals with disabilities can find assistance, often grants, by making accessibility modifications to their homes or workplaces. Funds for assistive devices are sometimes also available. Though not specifically grant related, a business owner may take a federal income tax credit for some of the costs of making accessibility improvements to the business that might benefit customers and/or employees.

Existing or prospective business owners should check with their local department of development, chamber of commerce, small business development centers, community action organizations, and any local workforce development agencies for information about assistance available in their area. Most business assistance is through favorable terms for financing, tax credits, or tax abatements for expansion projects. The amount of value of these may depend on the number of new people to be employed or retained or increases in income tax revenue to be generated. The amounts available can be substantial, in the range of tens or hundreds of thousands of dollars.

Low income individuals may qualify for small subsidized low interest loan programs, sometimes called microbusiness development programs. Home-based entrepreneurs might even find sweepstakes contests in which they might win funds, tuition, or equipment from magazines, office supply stores, or business equipment companies. The odds can be high, but someone has to win, and often the effort involved is quite small.

> **TIP:** *When entering sweepstakes, your information is prone to being distributed to other marketing "partners." To avoid disruptions from subsequent telemarketers, use a special free e-mail account as the contact e-mail (such as yahoo.com or hotmail.com). Also do not use your full name, or use a special pseudonym. Again, this will help you screen phone and mail and avoid disruptions from telemarketers. For your safety, never provide other personal or sensitive information such as your actual birthday, social security information, and driver's license number.*

Artists and writers can also find catalogs and Internet-based compendiums of financial assistance, scholarships, fellowships, and other merit- and need-based awards. Writers can access encouragement as well as links to writing contests, fellowships, and job lists at **www.fundsforwriters.com**. All artists should contact their state and local arts councils for possible awards or commissioned projects. Much like the not-for-profit world, they could compete for the opportunity to produce a commissioned work or work for a community arts program. Other ways to support your art and enhance your résumé and portfolio is to teach a community art class. Enter local art contests and volunteer to work with performance arts organizations to expand your repertoire and portfolio.

NETWORK SOURCES

Sometimes the most valuable information about grants and other forms of assistance comes by "word of mouth." Somebody knows somebody or has found a source that did not especially fit their needs, and eventually in casual conversation or by direct inquiry, you learn of the perfect opportunity for you. You and other members of your organization need to have contact with other professionals in your field or in your area for many reasons. This becomes part of your network. It is important to build time into your schedule to attend events and to establish contacts. This kind of "face time" is still critical to fostering the conversations that lead to the discovery and sharing of experiences. Learning from others' experiences is a shortcut to knowledge. Do not forget to be free in sharing your experiences with your contacts as well. Networking is a two-way flow of communication and help.

You develop a network through professional organizations that relate to your field. If none exist that have regular meetings and that are accessible to you, you may be able to locate a state or local roundtable of organizations that meets on a regular basis. These may be composed of a variety of nonprofits or other groups of related interests that serve a variety of needs in the community. Perhaps there is a local service organization, like the Rotary or Kiwanis, a church group, or a school booster organization. In any of these you have the opportunity to become friends with a number of people from different backgrounds. As the number of people you know increases, you will learn about more funding opportunities as well as other creative fund-raising techniques. As you learn of these, you are morally obligated to share your knowledge with others. This might seem to create more competition for the funds you are interested in winning, but generosity is always rewarded in kind. Through networking you learn to be a "giver" yourself.

About Requirements

In the process of applying for funds you should never challenge an agency's stated criteria with the intent of convincing it to change them. The board of the foundation has established its policies and grant award criteria. Only an action by the full board can make changes, and it may not do so without making such changes known and available to other potential applicants early in the grant cycle. In the case of government grants you should never implore your Congressperson or Senator to intercede on your behalf. Admittedly, most of them would be pleased to do so for you. However, most government grants have requirements that are codified in federal law and cannot be changed without changing the law — and that is beyond your reviewer's power. The grantor often uses an outside group of people under contract to review and rank applications according to a particular review format. In any case, you will place the reviewer, or your personal contact in the organization, in a difficult position, and you might very well be perceived as troublesome, which could severely injure your credibility in future grant applications.

Typical requirements might include restrictions to a particular geographic area. For example, community foundations restrict their awards to the local area; a corporation might restrict its awards to the area where it has facilities and has a presence. Some foundations review only proposals for which they have issued a specific invitation to an intriguing prospect to make an application. Funds are often restricted to a narrow range of uses, such as travel, research, educational expenses, underwriting of a special event, and production costs of a publication. There is more about requirements in Chapter 4.

CHAPTER SUMMARY

- Sources of grants

- Government
- Community foundations
- Private foundations
- Corporate donations or foundations

- Grant availability varies according to the prospective applicant.
    - Individuals
        - Artists
        - Writers
        - Teachers
        - Volunteers
        - Researchers
        - Homeowners, buyers, renters
    - Governments
    - Businesses
    - Nonprofits of nearly every type
- Catalogs of grants, scholarships, and business opportunities can be found at your library.
- Many catalogs and compendiums are also now available on the Internet as well.

- Professional and special-interest organizations often list opportunities in their newsletters.

- Attend agency-provided pre-proposal conferences.

- Target your search for grants according to the most likely sources for your needs.

- Refine your search according to the proportion of grant funding available and your total budget needs.

- Do not try to convince a funder to change its funding limits.

CHAPTER 4

WHAT DO THE GRANT MAKERS WANT & WHY?

CASE STUDY: AN

AN, quoted below, is an architect who volunteers as a grant reviewer for a Midwestern city's community foundation. It not only funds a number of arts, education, medical, and other worthy causes in the community, but also serves as a resource for local small family foundations. It assists them with investment decisions, helps them with running their grant cycles, funding choices, post-grant monitoring and even linking individual donors to foundations that match their interests.

"The foundation funds programs, not buildings and capital projects. The organizations funded should serve all people in the city. I serve on the committee that reviews smaller, incubator-type arts groups. When I first joined the committee, decisions were made in a very subjective manner. Our current executive director has since done an excellent job in developing a set of evaluation criteria with a numerical scoring formula to make sure each grant proposal was being evaluated fairly.

"Now the applications are filed electronically, and the applicant must respond to all the questions. There are many categories of questions that force the applicant to generate numbers: demographics of those they serve, the number they are able to serve, and descriptions of their outreach efforts. We also have an interview step. Lies and attempts to misrepresent data are usually pretty obvious and frowned upon. However, the fact that one organization might serve more people than another is not really a major criteria. We want to see that they have established a definite mission and plan for accomplishing it. We look for groups that serve a unique niche in the community arts spectrum. If there is no one else bringing chamber music into the schools, for example, or if no one else provides furnaces for glass blowing, if these activities might disappear without the efforts of this group, that is a major consideration in our funding."

— AN

The requirements for a proposal can be found in the guidelines you obtain from the corporation, foundation, or governmental unit. Sometimes the guidelines will even contain review criteria and ranking measures used to evaluate highly competitive grants. For example, they may describe their point system for ranking applications. The points they assign and the categories for assignment will vary according to their priorities and special interests. Therefore, a program that has a high priority for addressing childhood vaccinations in low income neighborhoods might assign more points to a community that has a higher percentage of low income households in the last census. Or it might assign more points to a program designed to reach out to a subgroup of the population that is shown to have lower levels of childhood immunizations. A ranking system might include a proportion of points for characteristics you have no control over, for example tied to the demographics of your community, mixed with some points for subjective criteria, such as merit and uniqueness of your approach. Grants to artists may have less-structured evaluation criteria, as in the case above: Does the artist demonstrate a high degree of accomplishment? Does the artist work in a unique medium? How does the artist help to promote appreciation for the arts? Does the artist have a following within the community? Make sure you have studied the requirements and can meet them before writing the application. If there are threshold requirements, be sure to demonstrate how you have met them. However, sometimes the requirements may be a little more obscure.

Just like an organization, a foundation or other funders have missions and goals that it wants to advance. It structures its funding decisions around proposals and organizations that closely match and can help advance its purpose in the community. Sometimes instead of overt statements about the types of proposals it supports, you must look more closely at its actual stated mission, goals, and the types of programs and organizations it has supported in the past.

Funders have differing preferences about the type of initial proposal you should submit. This book goes into detail about planning for, organizing, and preparing a long grant proposal. Many foundations prefer that you submit a letter of inquiry first, which allows them to assess your project's fit with their giving objectives, and then they may invite you to submit a long proposal. Government grants will often require that you submit a letter of intent in which you affirmatively state that you intend to respond to an upcoming solicitation for proposals. There are differences in the timing and content of each. How to prepare the Letter of Intent and the Letter of Inquiry can be found in Chapter 6.

CASE STUDY: DIANNE HARRIS

Reviewer Horror Story: Once a perfectly good proposal for home repair grant funds that I prepared was disqualified because the reviewer made a calculation error with regard to a threshold. It was a deceptively simple thing.

The threshold was to include photographs in the proposal, representing 10 percent of the homes in the target area. For a target area of 330 homes, one would include 33 photos. The reviewer simply miscounted. By the time the error was uncovered, that is, when I inquired as to why my application had come up short, all available funds had been committed to others and my project was just "out of luck, sorry" until the next year's round. From this I learned that you can never provide too much detail. The photos were even numbered clearly, but I could have included a statement with the actual calculation such as, "There are 330 homes in the target area shown. Ten percent of 330 is 33; therefore, there are 33 numbered photos in the following section." I could have included block maps, showing all 330 addresses.

— Dianne Harris

Take every opportunity to help the reviewer find everything in your proposal that is required or important to understanding the project. Some funders encourage the use of attachments and supporting documents, while others do not. Provide them with everything they ask for; number it, label it, annotate it — anything that will make your proposal clearer or more convincingly present the degree of need. However, do not include material that the guidelines specifically state should not be submitted, and watch that limits on length, if stipulated, are adhered to. With advances in technology, groups like to prepare videotape or compact disc presentations to reinforce their application. Some funders expressly encourage such presentations. However, not all funders have the time or equipment to review such presentations. They further may not review such information if they fear that the impact of the presentation might give an unfair advantage to an organization having the resources to create such material if others are not able to do so.

Again, pay close attention to the eligibility requirements of a grant and be sure that you do indeed qualify. They often cannot be changed.

CASE STUDY: DIANNE HARRIS

I once knew of a new company formed with the purpose of building new, affordable houses in a rural area. It approached a client of my company, the county commissioners, to apply for Community Development Block Grant funds to subsidize the cost of installing water lines to a site at the edge of a small town. They further convinced the county to apply for federal HOME investment opportunity funds through the State Department of Development, which would be used to provide low cost, down-payment loans to low income families who would purchase homes in the development.

Whether because of poor market analysis or weak execution, the company managed to sell only one house in the two-year period the subsidized down payments were available. Thus the county was found to have not met its program goal of assisting 15 low income families with new houses with the CDBG funds. The State Development Department was obligated by the U.S. Department of Housing and Urban Development (HUD) to pay back the money spent on extending the water lines.

During a crucial meeting the developer was given a chance to make a case that the funds were appropriately spent and with additional time, the goals would be met, thereby allowing the county to avoid having to repay the grant. However, the representative sent by the developer chose to ignore the script and instead challenged the Department of Development to change the rules for use of the HOME

CASE STUDY: DIANNE HARRIS

funds, because she was sure the homes would be very attractive to households with higher incomes and then would be easy to sell. Because this was not only not within the ability of a state agency, but also not within the parameters of use of the CDBG funds, the state was obligated to order the county to repay the funds. The county filed suit against the developer for the funds immediately.

— **Dianne Harris**

In this ill-fated case, the county was the legal grant recipient. Although it was depending on a reputable and knowledgeable developer to carry out a needed project, it was left "holding the bag" in the end and was responsible for the proper use of those funds, as well as meeting performance criteria. The developer further destroyed the county's only chance at avoiding a repayment by challenging the granting agency to change the underlying foundation for the use of HOME and CDBG funds to benefit and improve housing for low and moderate-income families. For this error, the developer partner lost the lawsuit and had to repay the county. There are several lessons to be drawn from this case, but for now accept that some rules cannot be changed, and it is worth finding out which ones cannot. It is far better to recognize that in the beginning and apply for funds whose criteria correspond with project plans.

CHAPTER SUMMARY

- Look for the funder's submission guidelines.
- Note the hints provided by other grant recipients or in catalogs.
- Research the target foundation — not just the grant program — to be able to more fully determine if the proposed program will be a good match to its interests.
- Guidelines may detail both format and content required.

- Assemble and provide any required attachments, documents, or data.
- Leave out anything expressly discouraged from submission.
- Do not attempt to implore them to change their requirements.

CHAPTER 5

GETTING ORGANIZED

As soon as a grant source is identified, it is important to mobilize the needed information and resources and organize them in a useful manner. It is a process similar to that of preparing an annual tax return — review the application requirements, and gather all data and documents together.

Just like in preparing taxes, original documents, materials, and information will be needed to document some of the requirements established by the funder and included in the proposal. There may be a deadline for submission of part or all of the proposal, and deadlines are firm. Of course all this must be done in addition to the "normal" workload. Some funders will want a great deal of source documentation, others very little. Be careful to include everything they specifically ask for, leave out anything they specifically instruct applicants to leave out, and be judicious about anything else. Sometimes the instructions will direct the applicant to place the material in the appendix, sometimes in separately tabbed sections, or sometimes at a specific place in the relevant section. The following checklist shows typical types of source documents that may be asked for. They include:

- Recent audit or financial reports
- IRS 501(c)(3) or other tax status determination
- Evidence of site control for building projects

  - Deeds, leases, option agreements
  - Map of site location

- Map of target area of service, if applicable, and other pertinent locations
- Determinations of zoning compliance
  - A letter from the local zoning office stating the use of the building proposed meets local law
- Commitment letters for other project funds
- Award letters for other project grants
- Certified cost estimates
- Board and staff résumés
- Board and staff licenses and certificates
- Letters of coordination from government or other nonprofit organizations
- Orders to make corrective measures from a regulatory agency
- Mission statement
- Annual plans (marketing and promotions, fund-raising, strategic, and capital improvements)

In recent years, letters of support from state and federal politicians or other non-involved organizations have become of declining importance and are of less interest than indications of coordinated effort with government or other private agencies.

HOW TO GET ORGANIZED, STEP-BY STEP

1. Starting with the guidelines, instructions, and any mandatory forms, make a backup copy. Those who are inclined to save paper may scan and store the material as an electronic file. One popular format is PDF (portable document format), and Adobe® Acrobat® is a popular program for creating these documents. Faxing the material to another office is an option. However it gets done, having duplicate material in a different physical location is an important emergency planning strategy. In the unfortunate event of a disaster, a company can save itself countless hours of recreating data and information, if it can be recreated at all, by taking this simple step.

2. Find any deadline dates. Do you have to provide a letter of intent prior to the proposal deadline? Will there be a grant information workshop? Is there a deadline for submitting questions?

3. Prepare a project management flow chart. This may be as simple as a hand-drawn chart, an inexpensive desktop calendar, or a computer-based project management software program.

- Research actual time to accomplish certain steps and, working backward, build time into your work plan to establish when to start each task.
- Take time to review submission requirements and to obtain the supplies you need: ink cartridges, paper, covers, bindings, dividers, and shipping supplies. Also have a good thesaurus and dictionary handy.
- Are resolutions required from the board authorizing the grant application or from a local governmental body to approve matching funds? When do they meet? How much lead time is needed to request time on its agenda? Does it require more than one meeting to review the request and made a decision? Perhaps all that is needed

is a letter from another entity, like the city's mayor. Still, make the request as soon as possible — there is a lot of competition for the grantor's attention.

TIP: *It is often helpful to draft a "sample" letter so that the end result will contain precisely the information that the funder requires, and it helps the person of whom the request has been made to complete the task more quickly.*

4. Then, working backward, start assigning dates to have each part of the proposal completed. Place all these deadlines on your calendar. Assign the "start by" dates. Chances are that, as the scheduling is worked out, it will become clear that the project is already behind schedule. Place this schedule in a highly visible area, and place tasks on the daily to-do list.

5. Resolve to make some progress every day. Chances are the request is for a significant sum of money. Although everyone may be busy with lots of other work, it is important to work toward successful completion and make a well-organized and convincing proposal a priority.

6. Start writing.

7. After the writing is completed, the time for production and shipping is a factor that should be accounted for in your schedule and planning:

TIP: *Even though the local copy center may advertise that it is open all night, the fact is that it may be backed up with other work, and sometimes different branches have different hours. This was a lesson I learned the hard way. I completed my long report at around 8 p.m., printed it out, and drove the original to the closest copy center, thinking it would run my copies overnight, that I would pick them up at 7 a.m., and that I would get to my 9 a.m. meeting just in time. Yes, it would be able to run the copies, but the branch would be closed from midnight until 9 a.m. Although* *my client was forgiving of my need to reschedule, the client was not happy, and it could have been disastrous. Two hours could mean the difference between an on-time submission or having the proposal returned unopened.*

- If mailing or shipping the proposal, check with a local shipper to verify its service. Depending on your location, the phrase "absolutely, positively overnight" may not apply. One advantage to paying extra for express or priority shipping is the ability to obtain proof of delivery. Also be sure that the delivery time will meet the deadline. A next-afternoon guarantee may not be good enough if the proposal is due by noon. Include a "ship-by" date in the writing schedule as well, incorporating a recommended time for the shipping vendor. Make sure the package will be ready well in advance of its "pickup" times.

- Likewise, if there is no choice but to personally deliver the proposal, leave adequate driving time. Be absolutely sure of the address for the delivery, where to park, and how to get there. Leave extra time for traffic. Even check the weather conditions along the entire route. In some cases, buildings have very tight security and only those "on the list" of authorized personnel will be allowed in. When hand-delivering a proposal package, try to get a timed and dated receipt for it from whomever it is left with. Once, years after submitting a proposal that was funded, the agency's auditor asked me to provide proof that I had submitted the proposal on time. I still had the receipt securely attached to my program records.

WRITING TIPS

TIP: *"I helped a friend prepare a grant application for funds to support an ESL (English as a Second Language) family-literacy program. It was satisfying because I was directly involved with the program as a tutor, and I knew first-hand the needs and the positive* *impact the program was making. Grant seekers can increase their chances of success by simple attention to detail. The application should be well-written, clear, and concise, with excellent and accurate documentation to support your needs and goals. The application needs to have an organized format that is easy to follow and understand. It is helpful to use easy-to-understand visual aids, such as maps, tables, and charts. Make sure you edit very carefully for clarity, grammar, spelling, and consistency of data. In a very competitive arena this can make a difference. Have one or two other people edit for you — they will catch things you miss."*

— JG

On Style

The writing style does not need to be poetry or great prose, but as JG observes, you should pay attention to the basics of grammar and spelling. Avoiding silly mistakes is more important than having special talent as a wordsmith. Those serving as editors of the proposal do not have to be especially skilled either. Often just having a fresh set of eyes to review the work is enough to catch inconsistencies and grammatical mistakes.

There are some other things to remember about wording. Time should not be wasted obsessing over finding the perfect wording. It is normal to get stuck looking for a word sometimes. Put down a phrase close to your intent, and better terminology can be substituted during the editing process. Do not overuse the same words or phrases. This obviously does not apply to names of actual methodologies, position titles, or other specific terms that must be used to ensure clarity. Get a good thesaurus or check for synonyms in the word processing program. Again, do not get hung up if something does not seem especially effective. The use of jargon may not be understood in the correct context or may be totally unfamiliar to the reader. Fully explain terms and concepts needed to describe the program to ensure the funder fully understands the point being made.

A grant proposal should be somewhat formal, rather than in a conversational tone. It should not be written in the first-person point of view, which may sound inappropriately familiar, but rather the third person. It is better to use the actual names of organizations or job titles. Do not use the pronouns I, we, or you, but refer instead to the XYZ Organization, the Feed the World Program, or the Good Money Foundation. Use the full name of the organization instead of abbreviations or acronyms. Similarly, avoid the use of slang or informal expressions. Also be careful to avoid the use of jargon common only in a particular industry. If terminology must be used that may not be commonly understood, be sure to explain each term. Footnotes may be used so that the flow of the narrative is not interrupted.

It is important to present a compelling case for your program or project, but that does not mean becoming maudlin or using overly emotional or contrived language. For example, instead of "The old post office building is the shining jewel of our community," you might try "The old post office building is known as an outstanding example of its architectural style." Knowledgeable sources can be cited as to the quality of the architecture, but "the shining jewel" is an unsubstantiated metaphor as well as a cliché.

Although the reader will be put off by the use of an exaggerated or overly wrought tone, it is desirable to create an emotional connection between the reader and the problem at hand. Use real-world examples, straightforward stories of actual clients, and how this program can or did improve their circumstances. But the story must provide specific information, not abstract adjectives. For example, to describe a patient of the J. M. McCoy Health Center example, one might say:

- "...due to pernicious poverty the family has been reduced to the public shame of abject begging in the streets..." (not very good)
- "...the family's poverty is a result of an inability to secure and retain steady employment. Like many others they have resorted to

panhandling to meet their most basic needs, even though it is illegal in our city." (better)

As examples, and as a comparison of two different styles of grants, two complete sample proposals are presented in the Appendix. One is to a fictional foundation by the "J. M. McCoy Health Center," and the other a fictional request for a small government grant, the "Microbusiness Development Program."

Getting Things on Paper

When all the preparation work is completed, then it is time to sit down and actually write the proposal. Writer's block can wreak havoc with the progress made in planning, organizing, and research. Start early and begin writing the proposal in the order it is to be presented. The following chapters present the typical arrangement of a grant proposal, with major parts discussed in separate chapters. Always refer often to any special instructions that the target foundation may provide. But if it does not stipulate a specific format, it is safe to use the model given in the next six chapters. These chapters provide a generic model that organizes the often required information into a logical, naturally flowing presentation. They will also cover how to write accessory pieces, letters of inquiry, or letters of intent, abstracts (or summaries), and cover letters. The rest of this chapter will provide more pointers on style and overcoming paralysis and procrastination.

Paralysis, Procrastination, and Time Management

Does this sound familiar? All the information has been assembled about the applicant organization and its program. All the steps of implementation have been thought out and detailed, and reliable cost estimates have been obtained. Dedicated research has led to the decision to approach a particular funder, and it appears to be the best fit to partner with for this project. However, even with the best information available, it can be disconcerting to know that so much is riding on this proposal. Perhaps due to timing, if this is not funded, there will not be another opportunity for as long as another year. Will the organization be able to survive until then? Will access to other opportunities be lost if this request is not funded right away? While staring at the glowing computer screen or a blank legal pad, it can be tough to think of a great start. It is easy to allow this insecurity to block the flow of constructive thinking. Thoughts may start racing, the phone may ring, interruptions may be dealt with, and suddenly one finds the day has gone without a word written. Too many of these days will doom the effectiveness of the final product.

It is time to master the discipline of proven time management techniques. For those who have not studied time management, some basic concepts are presented here.

Scheduling Tasks and Reminders

Some organizational tasks besides the actual writing will require the writer to "work" the project management schedule. Some tasks may be more difficult for some people. Some find it painful to pick up the phone and request a letter from someone. There may be extra steps in finding out who the right person is to contact for certain information in some communities. Placing such preliminary steps into the project management schedule and then forcing oneself to follow the steps will ensure nothing is forgotten. When prioritizing the day's "to do list" it may help to make the most difficult task the first thing to be accomplished for that day. The nagging specter of an unpleasant task drains energy and lessens effectiveness. However, being able to cross off a difficult task first can prove empowering and provide momentum for working on the next tasks. If there is only a specific window of time to reach a particular person, set a reminder alarm on your clock, cell phone, or computer. When it goes off, make the call. Use communication tools to their fullest capability and advantage. Leave messages or e-mails explaining what is needed, and convey that the request has a critical time component for a response. The message should indicate that a repeat contact will be made and when.

Once you have made contact and gotten agreement to provide the documents, letters, and other material required by your funder, it will be necessary to make follow-up contacts. Everyone is busy, and you are polite enough to want to not be a pest. However, other people's priorities are not the same as yours. It is a good idea to make a couple of polite reminder calls before you absolutely must have the document. That will bring it back to their attention and give you fair warning if the document cannot be obtained after all, for example if the supporter has changed his or her mind.

Other Time-Management Tricks

- It starts with commitment. Commit some part of the day to sitting in front of that blank page (or computer screen) without interruption. If possible, make that the time of day that provides the best opportunity to be most alert and creative. For some, that is the morning, before picking up anything else.

- Having something to drink close by may provide comfort. The aroma of a good cup of a special tea or a favorite coffee may help relax the spirit or stimulate thinking, allowing creativity to flow.

- Manage interruptions as much as your position allows. Phone calls can be directed into voice mail, doors should be closed if possible, and e-mails sent explaining when time will be available for other matters.

- If necessary and possible, it may be easier to avoid distractions by going to another place, such as the library, a corner conference room, or the local coffee shop. Laptop computers are popular for this purpose, but some still find it easier to write out ideas, or outlines, long-hand for later transcription.

- For others, "white noise," such as the soft buzz of conversation in a coffee shop, may be just what is needed. Others may use music, whether something a little peppy or soft and soothing, to get their brain into "the zone." The ideal workspace will contain the things that take the writer into a state where concentration is possible. However, be ready to change tactics if such preparations are being foiled by music turned too loud or if the conversations of others divert attention and interrupt the flow of ideas.

- Make use of little opportunities of time. Carry a notebook and jot down ideas that come to mind while waiting in the doctor's office or getting the car's oil changed. Inspiration can strike at unexpected times if you are open to it.

- Enlist others in the effort by asking them to do their part by reducing interruptions and running interference — like walking the dog, sorting the mail, and keeping the noise down outside the door. The organization, staff, volunteers, and program are dependent on this effort to achieve their goals. Everyone affected, staff, family, and dog, need to understand how important it is for the writer to have time to work on this extra project.

ORGANIZING IDEAS

Once you have all the ideas and information needed to write a convincing grant application, these thoughts have to be put into order. There have been several techniques developed to assist students and planners of any type to organize any sort of material. Two examples commonly used are the outline and the mind map. I find it helpful to produce the outline or mind map on large sheets of paper that get taped to a bulletin board over my desk.

Outlining

An excellent way to begin the writing process is to create an outline of the material. It does not have to be in quite the rigid outline structure taught in school. However, it does help to begin to get some words and ideas down on paper, organize their proper order, and think about how to develop a convincing and logical presentation of the proposed program. The typical framework of a proposal is often broken into several sections, in an order similar to the following list. This listing of sections, whether the typical format or in an alternative one defined by the funder, makes the most logical major headings for an outline.

1. Cover Letter
2. Project Abstract (or Summary)
3. Needs Statement
4. Program Description
5. Goals, Objectives, and Evaluation Plan
6. Organizational Background
7. Budget
8. Program Sustainability
9. Appendices

The next step is to go back and fill in the outline under each section in the following manner:

- Start with the most important point. Give supporting information. Summarize the paragraph.

- Next important point. Give supporting information. Summarize the paragraph.
- Continue with each major point until the story required in that section has been fully developed.
- Revise the outline. Should anything be added? Are there key ideas or phrases that should go in certain places? Insert them.

Mind-mapping

Mind-mapping uses a more graphical and less linear way to organize material. It places the central idea of the writing into a large circle (or any shape representing your theme — such as a house or a heart) in the center of the worksheet. Three to five supporting thoughts that develop the central idea radiate out from it. They are connected to the central idea with lines and arrows that by direction can illustrate the flow of influence. More supporting ideas radiate from the others, and more lines connect and interconnect these to others. The use of color to separate themes, or even the heaviness of the lines can help to distinguish items of greater importance. The ideas are sorted into the most logical development of the entire piece. Each idea is developed into a sentence at its appropriate place in the narrative, as listed in the mapping exercise. Graphically and visually oriented people find this type of process helpful and even stimulating to creative thought.

Starting with organizing techniques like these, linking the thoughts together in a hierarchical manner, the language of the narrative should begin to flow naturally. This process may feel tedious when starting, especially if it is unfamiliar, but systematically organizing the material nearly automates the actual writing and makes it easier to complete. It especially helps to guarantee that no important information has been accidentally left out.

Other Considerations of Organization

In some cases, someone who does not know the organization well may want to make the request in writing. Prepare and deliver that written request, again explaining exactly what is needed and why. A real time-saver can be to provide example language or a sample document for the writer to refer to, as well as sources where he or she can do research into the organization or the target funder if desired. Give him or her every reason to know that the request and program are legitimate and support will not potentially reflect poorly on the writer. It is always best to try as much as possible through networking to have a prior established relationship with those who will be needed for support. See Chapter 1.

Working late into the night or waiting until the last minute are not good strategies for producing effective proposals. Although some time outside the normal day might be necessary, start on an earlier calendar date. Bodies and brains need rest to produce their best work. Studies have shown that reaction times of the sleep-deprived are the same as those who are impaired by alcohol. Grant writers cannot be at their best, their most enthusiastic, or their most effective if they try to work when completely exhausted. Leave the all-nighters to college students. To create an award-winning proposal, the grant writer must be in an enthusiastic frame of mind and be able to convey that to the reader.

We have not yet achieved a "paperless" society. It can be a time-saver to safely store original documents or letters gathered and have backups. I like to use a fresh file folder, labeled for the particular grant program, with the material secured by a "binder" clip.

Likewise, if you are inclined to eat at your desk, it is best to avoid messy, greasy foods. Better yet, it is better to take short breaks as scheduled and consume snacks or meals at some distance from the grant materials and tools or even get away from the office. Fresh air and a change of scenery can help to refresh the mind and loosen up the muscles. Feelings of being tapped out, tired, headachy, or stiff are signs the body needs to rest or at least engage in something different for a while. In short, successful grant writers take steps to secure materials and tools, work diligently, and also take care of their own health.

Consider the potential for disasters. Electrical power systems have a strange way of surging and failing when one is working on something really important. The cleaning staff can inadvertently knock a stack of paper into the wastebasket at night. The information technology (IT) department may decide that today is a great day to defrag the system, and for some reason some or all if it will not work now. The idea is to attempt to be prepared for anything at the worst possible time. Back up everything and back up often. Make extra copies to store somewhere else. If working at a computer, use a backup drive, CD, or a portable storage device, such as "flash drives." They are easy to use and small enough to fit in a shirt pocket or small purse; however, older computers may not be compatible or not have the correct connection (Universal Serial Bus, USB) for these devices. Another alternative method for backing up files is to e-mail the file to one's own e-mail account each day, allowing the data to be stored on a server if it happens to be needed later. Internet-based file storage systems also exist, and if one happens to already be available, use it as an excellent alternative. At any rate, a great deal of time and effort will be invested in creating the document, and in the event of an emergency, it can be a project saver to have some way to recover the work quickly.

CHAPTER SUMMARY

- Develop a project control system (checklist) as soon as a grant is identified.
- Back up all material in an off-site location in the event of disaster.
- Identify all deadlines.

- Identify all steps that must be completed and their deadlines. A sample grant writing schedule appears in the Appendix.
- Begin requests for letters of support or verification of coordinated action as soon as possible.
- Identify and gather all supporting information and documents requested.
- Allow sufficient time for "production," copying, binding, and shipping.
- Find a comfortable place to work on the proposal.
- Assemble the right tools.
- Make sufficient time to work on the proposal.
- Choose a reasonable time of day to work on the proposal.
- Make this work a daily priority.
- Get help with proofreading; do not let silly mistakes slip through.
- Be concise but clear.
- Use a formal tone, not conversational.
- Use a third-person voice, not a familiar first-person voice.
- Avoid the use of acronyms or abbreviations.
- Avoid the use of jargon.
- Use visuals effectively.
- Avoid exaggerations and generalizations.

- Work with your checklist or project management sheet in plain view.
- Create an outline.
- Revise and fill in the outline.
- Finish the narratives.
- Take precautions.
- Store materials together and securely.
- Back up computer files.
- Take care of physical and mental health.

Section

The Parts of a Grant Application

CHAPTER 6

FIRST CONTACT

Once a grant opportunity has been targeted, you will make initial contact in some way. Even if grant guidelines and instructions are easily available via Internet, many grant makers require some form of initial contact. For some others you will be required to make a personal contact, maybe by phone to request an application package. Whenever possible you should try to connect with someone in the funding organization to provide it with advance information and create awareness of your project and desire to apply for its funds, such as informally through your network. However, an applicant should be respectful of a funder that specifically instructs applicants to not make direct initial contacts.

The two most commonly required contacts are either the letter of intent or the letter of inquiry. Sometimes even these are requested to be submitted electronically in either a narrative or form-based format.

THE LETTER OF INTENT

The letter of intent is brief, perhaps only one page, and simply declares your intention to apply for a specific program. Mention it by name; tracking number; category, if the funder has more than one category in which it will be making awards; the name of the actual applicant; and contact information for the applicant.

The letter of intent allows the funder, often a governmental grantor, to gauge the number and types of applications it can expect, so that it can adjust staffing and workloads. It has requirements for the amount of time available for review, so that funds can be expended in accordance with budgetary cycles. Only submit a letter of intent if it is specifically requested or required. There is often a deadline for submission for the letter as well, and if not submitted, you may not be eligible for the application submission.

Note: *The following is a fictitious proposal. Neither the organization nor the staff members exist. Any similarity to actual persons or organizations is coincidental. However, the format is intended to demonstrate an effective method of submitting a proposal to a foundation for a human services activity.*

SAMPLE LETTER OF INTENT

Ralph S. Jones, Administrator
Alzheimer's Center of the Midwest, LLC
11111 Pittman Ave.
Columbia, OH 43200

January 1, 2007

Mr. J. Donald
Victor Donald Foundation
44444 Pittman Ave.
Columbia, OH 43200

RE: Dementia Care Innovations Grant
Notice of Funding Availability: #2007-0200-005
dated: November 2, 2006

Dear Mr. Donald:

This letter is to advise the Victor Donald Foundation of our intent to apply for the new Dementia Care Innovations Grant in the upcoming competitive application round due February 15, 2007. This Letter of Intent is in response to the instructions issued with the grant Notice of Funding Availability issued November 2, 2006.

SAMPLE LETTER OF INTENT

The Alzheimer's Center of the Midwest, LLC, a subsidiary of Alzheimer's Care Centers of America, will be the applicant for the Dementia Care Innovations Grant. We may be reached for additional information at the above address in care of Mr. Ralph S. Jones, Administrator, or by phone at 999-388-8226.

Thank you for the opportunity to apply for these important funds.

Sincerely,

Ralph S. Jones, Administrator
Alzheimer's Care Center of the Midwest, LLC

THE LETTER OF INQUIRY

The letter of inquiry should be sent only if requested or required. It is a longer letter, perhaps up to four pages, that briefly describes:

- Your program
- Your organization
- The goals of the program
- Other fund-raising efforts and their success
- A short description of the project budget
- Any other information that may be outlined in the funder's guidelines

This letter does not request a specific amount of money but only requests the opportunity to submit a full proposal and perhaps the opportunity to meet with the funder to discuss the merits of your project. Again, make sure you meet any deadlines for submission and that you are clear about how long the funder will take to act on a letter of inquiry. When letters of inquiry are required, do not submit a long proposal until you have been invited.

The letter of inquiry allows the foundation or corporation to review your organization and proposed program for consistency with their goals without them having to go through great volumes of information on a potentially un-fundable project. It also allows you to save a great amount of effort on proposals that really would not have had a chance. However, with a good job of strategically researching your potential benefactors and designing a well-thought-out program and a concise and effective presentation, your letter of inquiry should meet with success.

If the funder provides guidelines, review them thoroughly for information about submission requirements, proposal organization, timing of a funding round, details about required information, and specifics about the types of projects it is seeking proposals for. Then carefully follow all instructions. Use all required forms and provide the required level of detail. Letters of inquiry for highly competitive grants will be set aside without being reviewed if thresholds or organizational requirements are not met.

Some federal agencies employ outside staff to review the letters for some grant programs. These reviewers use highly standardized evaluation tools and have almost no room for discretion concerning how to rate proposal elements. This may even extend to the use of specific terms and phrases as presented in their guidelines so that a reviewer unfamiliar with your field will not eliminate your request because he or she did not recognize a term as an equivalent. In these cases, it is extremely important to follow and use their provided format, forms, and instructions to be sure that all your proposal components are easily recognized as those that are required.

Note: *This is a fictitious proposal. Neither the organization nor the staff members exist. Any similarity to actual persons or organizations is coincidental. However, the format is intended to demonstrate an effective method of submitting a proposal to a foundation for an educational activity.*

SAMPLE LETTER OF INQUIRY

Backwoods River Nature Center
100 River Ave.
Columbia, OH 43200

January 1, 2007

Ms. June Forester
Natural Resources Alliance
200 Lake Ave.
Columbia, OH 43200

Dear Ms. Forester:

The founding Board of the Backwoods River Nature Center is writing to inquire about your interest in supporting a new educational initiative of the Backwoods River Nature Center. This is a program initiative serving the students of the Columbia Public Schools. This will be a program that will provide instructional resources in middle school classrooms for a new natural science and environmental studies unit. The unit has been designed with the objective of integrating math, science, reading, and writing skills into a cross-functional and interdisciplinary approach. The unit is designed to provide students with the skills to meet 8 of 15 requirements of the ninth grade proficiency test in mathematics, 10 of 12 requirements of the ninth grade proficiency test, and to reinforce reading and writing skills that are required at this grade level.

The unit will also include presentations about the ecology of the Backwoods River Basin and the geologic and human history of the Basin. Students will visit the nature center once each grading period for field survey work. In-school laboratory projects and demonstrations will include replicating natural processes of erosion, observing the impacts of reduced dissolved oxygen on aquatic plants, and the life cycles of insects native to the Basin. Math skills developed will include metric measurements and conversions, organizing data into tables and graphical analysis as well as computations of expected and actual results of lab exercises. Students will read the results of research into similar river basin ecologies. They will write two term papers, one at the midpoint of the year about their literature search, and one at the end of the year about their conclusions after completion of the laboratory work and mathematical analysis.

SAMPLE LETTER OF INQUIRY

The mission of the Backwoods River Nature Center is to provide experience-based learning about nature and the Backwoods River Basin. A secondary benefit of the Nature Center and its management of the grounds is the protection of the stream and provision of passive recreation opportunities for the community.

The founding board is made up of business leaders and environmental professionals who have witnessed the toll of poor resource management resulting in flooding and loss of species diversity in the last century. The schools have approached us to assist them in creating an experiential curriculum that will help their students meet the requirements of the state-mandated proficiency tests, particularly in the fields of science and mathematics. Thus this program was developed by a blue-ribbon panel of science and math teachers and park rangers at the Nature Center.

The community has responded enthusiastically to the project with volunteers and donations of transportation for the students. In order to complete the launch of the project, we require funding for printing specialized curriculum materials and study guides and to acquire special laboratory equipment and supplies for the in-school laboratory study. If invited to present a full proposal, the Nature Center will request $140,000 to meet the cost of a one-year program for an estimated 700 students.

We appreciate your consideration of our program and look forward to the opportunity to meet with you to further discuss this request and the work of the nature center. For more information please feel free to contact me, Jeff Skinner, at 614-386-8115. Thank you for your consideration.

Sincerely,

Jeff Skinner, Executive Director
Backwoods River Nature Center

BEGINNING THE MAIN APPLICATION DOCUMENT: COVER LETTERS AND SUMMARIES

The Cover Letter

Every grant proposal needs an introductory statement. Although it appears first, the cover letter is written last. When the application is complete, the cover, or transmittal, letter is written and attached to the beginning or outside, of the application package. The cover letter, sometimes called the letter of transmittal, is a short statement of who you are, how to contact you, why you are applying, which program you are applying to, and the amount of the request. It is a formal letter that should be typewritten on letterhead stationery and be hand-signed by the chief officer of the organization (or yourself if an individual). It should be limited to a single page. Copies of the cover letter can appear behind, or instead of, a title page on each copy of the proposal, depending on the length. Very short proposals may not need a title page. The sample cover letter at the end of this chapter can serve as a template for other grant requests.

The Project Summary

Most grants require a summary, sometimes called an abstract or a synopsis, which provides the most pertinent information about the organization, the program proposal, and the funds being requested and is limited to just a few pages. Some funders, including government grants, will provide one or more forms indicating the information they wish to have in the abstract, which simply needs to be filled out and attached. If no preset forms are provided, the sample at the end of this chapter can serve as a template for setting up a synopsis to introduce the applicant and its grant request.

The program summary will very briefly present the major facts of the proposal. It will repeat the name of the grant program for which you are applying, as many funders have more than one program. It will describe the reason for the request, the identified need, the project concept, and the location of the project for which you want funding. It will describe your unique ability to carry out the project and list the major goals of the project. It will include the estimated costs of the project, the total cost, the grant request amount, and how funds for the difference will be obtained. It will provide contact information for key people associated with the grant request.

A very long proposal may also include a table of contents, listing the page numbers of each section. The summary appears after the table of contents or, in a short proposal, after the cover letter.

Samples of project summaries are found in the sample proposals that follow here and in the Appendix.

CASE STUDY: HOPE FOR NEW LIFE

The Hope for New Life organization, mentioned in Chapter 1, will serve throughout the book as our case study of what not to do. A hypothetical grant application for them has been created, as if they had written it for themselves. Each section of the hypothetical application will be presented in the chapter addressing the corresponding section. It will be contrasted with a sample that is a more effective approach, and the weaknesses of the Hope for New Life example will be pointed out in the case study analyses.

From the hypothetical application for Community Development Block Grant funds submitted by Hope For New Life,
a social service agency serving Some Town, Ohio

A. Project Summary

The Hope for New Life organization has been created to provide a comprehensive and multifaceted solution to the challenge of ending poverty and reliance on welfare in our community. Our approach is inspired by the welfare reform initiatives of the early 1990s, which placed time limits for receiving welfare benefits and required recipients to enter into educational or training programs to prepare them to enter the workforce by the time their benefits period expires.

The new rules have taken effect without consideration for whether there exist enough education, training, and employment resources within a community to serve the large number of people receiving welfare. Hope for New Life will provide a training resource to help fill that gap for the residents of Some Town.

Our request for the city's Community Development Block Grant Fund (CDBG) allocation of $9,000,000 is large but will be a one-time expense to the city. In addition to allowing us to set up and begin running our programs, it will.

CASE STUDY: HOPE FOR NEW LIFE

allow us to set up an endowment that will provide the needed funds to operate the organization in perpetuity, without future requests for money.

Our proposed methodology addresses two of the major drawbacks to forcing young, single welfare mothers into the workforce. First of all, our town and its employment opportunities are widely spread out and without complete access by public transportation. Most of our welfare recipients also cannot afford private cars to get to a workplace that might be able to hire them otherwise. Second of all, child care is very expensive, and most centers already have full enrollment. Therefore, Hope for New Life proposes to provide the following services: 1) To provide child care for the single mothers who enroll in our training programs. 2) The child care facility will provide a training option as future child care providers for some the enrollees. 3) There will be an training facility teaching automotive repair. It will provide real work experience by using donated older autos. When those autos are repaired, they will be given to the program graduates so that they will have reliable transportation to their new jobs. 4) There will be classes for our enrollees to study for and obtain their General Education Diploma (GED), which is recognized as a high school equivalency anywhere. This alone will qualify many welfare recipients to obtain jobs.

Hope for New Life consists of educational professionals that are fully qualified to serve adult educational needs. When our funding is secured, we will be able to secure space for our training facilities, begin enrollments, and hire the necessary additional staff to serve the number of applicants who enroll with us.

Hope for New Life can be contacted through the Executive Director, Ralph Hope, at 333 Out There Lane, Some Town, OH, 40004. Our phone is 999-111-2222.

Analysis: Hope for New Life's program summary, above, includes most of the discussion points that you should include in a program summary, but it contains a number of flaws. A major one is that it has not thoroughly researched the Community Development Block Grant Program. It does not allow for the establishment of endowments. Neither has Hope For New Life taken into account the fact that the community funds a vast number of important activities and capital projects with the CDBG program. More than likely, the city has established policies for the dollar amount that is available for applicant community organizations, and these have not been investigated. Regardless of what the council person may have told the group, it is really not likely that these other projects would be abandoned for a year in favor of giving the entire allocation to a single entity. The summary is also too short. More detail about the program and the applicant should be given. Of course in this case, those details don't exist, so they couldn't be presented. A more effective program summary can be examined at the end of the chapter.

Note: *The following is for a fictitious proposal. Neither the organization nor the staff members exist. Any similarity to actual persons or organizations is coincidental. However, the format is intended to demonstrate an effective method of submitting a proposal to a foundation for a human services or cultural activity.*

SAMPLE COVER LETTER

Jones Dance Company
100 Main Street, Columbia, OH 43200
Telephone: (999) 888-7777 Fax: (999) 888-7778 E-mail: happyfeet@internet.org

Mr. John Smith, Grant Review Coordinator
The My Town Foundation
P.O. Box 0000
Columbia, OH 43200

January 1, 2007

Dear Mr. Smith:

Attached is a request for funding from the Jones Dance Company, a newly organized community dance troupe. The staff and volunteers of the dance company have raised a significant amount of community support for its service to the low income community through free live performances and dance instruction for teenagers in Columbia, Ohio. However, the Jones Dance Company still faces a shortage of $15,000 for its first-year budget to rent rehearsal and performance space. Because of the My Town Foundation's interest in improving cultural opportunities and engaging youth in creative activities in low income neighborhoods, the Jones Dance Company hopes that the foundation will provide a grant for the needed funds.

Please feel free to contact me at any time to address any additional questions you may have. You may reach me by any of the means listed above.

Thank you for your consideration.

Sincerely,

Joy LaFeet, Artistic Director/Grant Contact

SAMPLE SYNOPSIS (SUMMARY) SHEET AND ABSTRACT

Grant Request from the My Town Foundation

by the Jones Dance Company

Synopsis:

Grant Contact: Joy LaFeet

Artistic Director: Joy LaFeet

Staff:

- 1 part-time paid Artistic Director
- 1 part-time Music Director
- 15 volunteers
- 5-person board of directors

Tax Status:
The Jones Dance Company is tax exempt per IRS Section 501(c)(3).

Request for Funding:
$15,000 (though any support will be appreciated)

Type of Organization:
Community Arts

Service Area:
Mill Quarter Neighborhood and Mill County

Target Population Served:
Primarily residents of Mill Quarter Neighborhood but with a growing audience

Mission:
To provide access to cultural and creative expression to members of our low income community, enriching and inspiring their lives.

Abstract:
There is great need for quality youth programming and cultural events in low income neighborhoods in Columbia, Ohio, particularly the Mill Quarter neighborhood which is plagued by gang activity and unemployment. The city's parks and recreation centers provide programming directed at elementary-age children and the elderly but have nothing to offer for teens and young adults.

SAMPLE SYNOPSIS (SUMMARY) SHEET AND ABSTRACT

The low income families have been shown to be more likely to be affected by health conditions that have links to stress, such as obesity, diabetes, high blood pressure, and high cholesterol. Bored teens with little adult supervision outside of school are prey for gangs and more prone to commit legal offenses, engage in premature and unprotected sexual activity, and have lower grades compared to teens that have stimulating activities to channel their energy. The low income families have little opportunity to engage in activities that challenge them in a positive way, activities that would enable them to enjoy success and empowerment and increase their self-esteem.

Creative expression, especially forms like dance, which has the added benefit of being a physical activity, has been shown to be a vehicle for reduction of stress, an outlet in which to channel strong emotions in a not-damaging way, and a unifying force for a community. Exposure to the arts stimulates brain activity and community interaction.

The Jones Dance Company is a new offering in the city and the first of its type in this neighborhood. It will provide lessons to interested teens in the school gymnasium. They will be encouraged to learn, create, and present dance recitals as well as have the opportunity to attend professional works of classical and modern dance. The director and board members all have extensive experience in the arts, administration, and in serving culturally diverse populations.

Several members of the community have joined the effort to create this program, including existing visual arts organizations, the local business community, local colleges, the Columbia Metropolitan Ballet, sewing clubs, and community churches. The company needs to be able to rent performance space, rehearsal space, and space to construct and store sets and costumes. The schools are unable to provide this amount of space and are not available when the school term is not in session. Area churches have provided some performance space in the past, but audience attendance has grown beyond the capacity of local churches, averaging more than 250 attendees for each of four professional performances each year. A restored historic movie theater is in the district and would make a perfect home for the Jones Dance Company. The additional financial support of the My Town Foundation will help make this facility a reality.

CHAPTER 7

WHAT NEEDS FIXING? THE NEEDS STATEMENT

CASE STUDY: HOPE FOR NEW LIFE

The hypothetical application from Hope for New Life is revisited, by examining the shortcomings of the needs statement portion of its application. A more effective sample will follow later in the chapter.

From the hypothetical application for Community Development Block Grant Funds submitted by Hope For New Life, a social service agency serving Some Town, Ohio

B. Statement of Need

Hope for New Life's approach is inspired by the federal welfare reform initiatives of the early 1990s, which limited receiving welfare benefits to a period of only 24 months and required recipients to enter into educational or training programs to prepare them to enter the workforce by the time their benefits period expired. Hope for New Life wants to address these causes of poverty for the entire city and will need substantial funds to build a program of that size. An established endowment for future operations will allow the staff to devote all its efforts on serving the poor, rather than constantly spending time on fund-raising.

The new rules have taken effect without consideration for whether there exist enough education, training, and employment resources within a community to serve the large number of people receiving welfare. Hope for New Life will provide a training resource to help fill that gap for the residents of Some Town. The new rules also provide little exception for those who may have undiagnosed disabilities that

CASE STUDY: HOPE FOR NEW LIFE

underlie their inability to work. These requirements put a large number of recipients at risk when their benefits expire and they may have not yet secured appropriate employment. There is also some question as to whether the jobs they attain will provide a living wage or health benefits.

Especially in the case of unwed mothers, many dropped out of high school in order to care for their young children, and the lack of a high school diploma prevents them from becoming employed at many companies. Without contributions from the absent fathers, the mother cannot really support her growing family any other way than through public assistance. The cost of long-term public assistance, including healthcare, usually rent assistance, and food stamps is very expensive to our nation. That is why the "Welfare-to-Work" initiatives were created.

There are other major drawbacks to forcing young, single welfare mothers into the workforce. First of all, our town and its employment opportunities are widely spread out and without complete access by public transportation. Most of our welfare recipients also cannot afford private cars to get to a workplace that might be able to hire them otherwise. Second of all, child care is very expensive, and most centers already have full enrollment. Another child care-related issue is that no professional child care providers offer care beyond standard day shift hours. Many companies are transitioning to 24-hour service and often require newer employees to cover the second- or third-shift operations.

There is need for employment for many young men in the community as well. There are very few job training opportunities for young men who are no longer attending public schools. The state's general assistance cut out able-bodied men years ago. When unemployed, they may double up living quarters with family or friends. If they lack social skills or have substance abuse issues, they are at risk of living on the streets. Hope for New Life would welcome these young men into its high school equivalency program and auto mechanics training program.

Recent newspaper articles have told how today's employers need skilled workers and the public schools and existing social service network have failed to ensure that young people receive the education and training they need to be successful in life and in the workplace. The declining welfare assistance places many of those in poverty at extreme risk of not living a decent life and further reduces their abilities to raise themselves out of poverty unless the complicating factors of their lives are also addressed.

Analysis: In the case of the Hope for New Life organization, it had conceived of an interesting and multifaceted approach to address poverty with

CASE STUDY: HOPE FOR NEW LIFE

education, job training, child care, and transportation. Its needs statement, in addition to other weaknesses, however, presents no firm evidence of the extent of poverty in its community or even if the barriers it alleges are the real contributing factors to economic security for those who might be experiencing poverty. The organizers were constructing a program to address the poverty of single mothers with young children. However, in some communities, those who suffer most from poverty are the elderly and handicapped. The representative could not tell me the proportion of single mothers to the total impoverished population of the community, how many households were affected, if they were concentrated in particular neighborhoods, or anything that amounted to actual data or experience with whether this was an appropriate program for this community. He had not consulted with the welfare office, other job training programs, or single mothers who needed jobs. There was just no firm evidence to present to the reviewing committee about the need for this program. Now in fact, when writing its grant the group could have taken responsibility for researching and presenting the facts needed to support the case. But when the executive director was advised to do this, he was annoyed and insisted that such research was unnecessary, would take too much time, and deflected his efforts from the important work he needed to do. Often grant seekers feel that way. The ones who feel that way, like Hope for New Life, do not receive their funding.

In contrast, when a small city in the northern part of our state wanted to improve the restroom facilities at its softball fields, it documented a clear need for the request. First of all, federal legislation requires that all public facilities be accessible to people with handicaps. The old restrooms at the city-owned park were constructed long prior to this legislation and had stalls and wash stand areas that were too small to get a wheelchair into, did not have grab bars, and were missing other requirements. The law was clearly documented; the city group had drawings showing the dimensions and layout of the restrooms as well as drawings showing the required dimensions and the most feasible layout that would comply with the law. They had collected census data about the number of adults and children in the community with mobility impairments. They had collected data on the numbers of users in the park every year and broken it down by several categories, including participants in the softball leagues. From there they were able to project the number of people who would now be able to attend and participate in events at the park if the restroom modifications were constructed. All the data added up to a clearly documented need and receipt of thousands of dollars in matching grant money to modernize the restrooms at the softball fields.

Another more effective sample of a needs statement appears at the end of the chapter.

This chapter addresses how to write an effective needs statement. The needs statement is the first detailed narrative to be written and may be the most important section. The program synopsis or summary may appear first, but the needs statement sets the stage for why the proposed project or program was created and why anyone would want to fund it. This chapter will cover ways to make a compelling case for a project by thoroughly describing and quantifying the need that has been identified. It will show how to effectively use statistics, facts, studies, graphs, tables, and real-life stories to organize data and to help tell a convincing story.

Comparing the two organizations in the previous case study analysis, it should be clear which is more likely to be funded. Although the first group may actually have a substantial need to address, it did not appear to have given it any real thought. The funder is not going to look up statistics on the magnitude of a problem for the applicant, and the funder's assumptions and experience with the needs of the community may be entirely different than those in the applicant's community. In the second case, the staff of the parks department had been keeping records over a period of time, staying informed of new legislation, consulting with advocacy groups for the handicapped, and had already researched the parameters of the proposed restroom improvements. The group knew the size of the problem in the community and how much effort was needed to make a reasonable impact on improving the recreation program for the handicapped in its community. The first group seemed to be making things up as it went along; the second had done research and could prove the requested funds would be effectively used.

The needs statement is the place to thoroughly describe the problem that has been identified. How did this problem come to light? Is there evidence that it has existed for some time, or is it a result of some recent upset in the community? Are there sources or studies that can be cited that present the problem in this community or in other places? Compare and contrast the situation in this community versus what is being found in other places.

Can the proposed program fix the cause of the problem or specific events or situations in a way that can be documented? Perhaps it is possible to quantify the increase in negative impact or decrease in desirable features that occurred after the event or change in the community.

The needs statement will quantify the current extent of the problem. How many people are affected? Is the problem becoming greater? How much does this problem cost, expressed in terms the reader can easily understand? Are there measurable impacts on lost work time or productivity, incidence of health problems, medical costs, graduation rates, incarceration rates, the costs of incarceration, or perhaps the cost of lost opportunities?

Demographics are characteristics summarized by statistics that describe the population of people most affected by a problem or living in a particular neighborhood. Demographics involve parameters, such as the number of people in an area, type and amount of income, where they work or go to school, and other measures of wealth, educational attainment, age, numbers of people in a household, and ethnic identities. Demographic information and comparisons lend themselves well to organization in table formats or graphs for ease of comparison and for tracking changes over time. The largest single collector of demographic data is the United States Department of Commerce during the decennial census of population. Unique collections of Census Bureau information are periodically published by the Bureau, including the City and County Data Book and the North American Industry Classification System (NAICS), which is used to categorize data from detailed industrial and occupational sectors. Many local governments report their most recent census as well as any estimated changes for the period between the last census and the current date as part of their annual financial report. Local governments sometimes also conduct periodic surveys of citizen attitudes, including some demographic information that can be useful for detailed and up-to-date information. These may be published and made available in the local library, distributed to the city council and other community leaders, and on its Web site. The local

Board of Realtors and Chamber of Commerce may provide community profiles and market data to their members as well as in media releases and marketing materials, which may include population and economic data gathered from many sources, including their own surveys. Many retailers and other companies conduct various consumer surveys that almost always contain some demographics in their data. These tend to be proprietary but can sometimes be accessed from a company's Web site or in its annual report. Any member of your board of trustees may have access to data gathered in specific ways by one's primary business that he or she can make available to you. The U.S. Department of Commerce also includes the National Technical Information Service, which publishes a number of data reports. Its Web site, **www.ntis.gov**, provides access to a number of its and other government data publications. Though free information is readily available, there are fee-based services that also provide this material already formatted and that will sometimes provide customized comparisons of communities. The U.S. Census demographic information is also available via its Web site, **www.census.gov**. Many localities also reproduce the most recent census information for their towns on their official Web site as a marketing tool but which is available to anyone interested in the community. Other sources of data for your community includes other economic development organizations, regional planning commissions, your State or County Department of Development, and local colleges or universities. Other nonprofit organizations and school districts may have and share data about the community as well as about the level of need or costs related to their areas of specialty.

The U.S. Census Bureau also conducts a census of business activity every five years, those ending in "2" or "7," and compiles that information into the Economic Census (also available on **www.census.gov**), and the U.S. Department of Labor, Bureau of Labor Statistics (**www.bls.gov**) publishes data related to employment and unemployment trends at the national, state, and county level. These can be used to gain insights into employment trends, consumer behavior, and regional economic facts. For international information the Central Intelligence Agency (CIA) publishes the World Fact Book, a reference manual of data on more than 260 nations and other entities, complete with a set of maps. International aid groups as well as local social service agencies also collect and disseminate data about the issues, countries, and people that they serve. You might even be able to generate statistics about your clientele from your records that will be especially informative about the unique conditions affecting your constituents.

> **TIP:** *Be careful to attribute your statistics properly through footnotes or endnotes. Note who compiled the data, the name of the publication, the date of publication, the place of publication, and page(s) where the fact(s) appeared.*

Be sure to describe clearly any special circumstances about how study data was gathered. The conclusions drawn about the study group may not apply to your target population. Be sure to understand and highlight the significant similarities or differences.

A few well-placed tables and charts can convey a point quickly and sometimes more clearly than long narratives. It is true that a picture is worth a thousand words. Using tables and charts can be especially helpful if a proposal is required to be brief per the guidelines. Be sure graphs and charts are well annotated and accurately labeled and that they cite the source and age of data. Simple tables can be created in most word processing programs. Integrated office suite programs have spreadsheet programs that can be used to create a table and translate the data into various simple graphs, which can then be inserted into the compatible word processor program.

The following examples show three examples of presentation of the same hypothetical data. The data set, which is the age distribution of fictional This City in the year 2000 and 2007, can be presented in a table, a pie chart, or in a 3-D bar chart. Note the two sources of data from 2000 and 2007 are cited. Tables allow large amounts of information to be organized and to show precise numbers. Charts allow the data to be perceived in proportions, and with appropriate labels or accompanying tables, the data is readily understandable.

THIS CITY, AGE DISTRIBUTION TABLE, 2000-2007		
Age Group	Ages in 2000	Ages in 2007
	Total #	Total #
< or = 25	17	85
26-35	91	88
36-45	89	80
46-55	75	85
56-65	58	45
Over 65	74	61
Totals	404	444
*Sources: U.S. Census of 2000 and Community Survey of 2007		

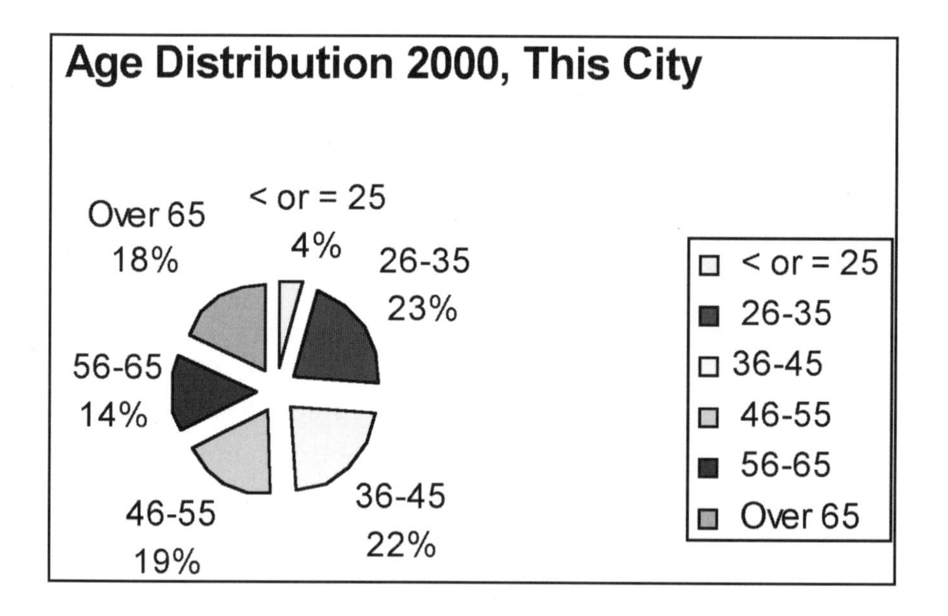

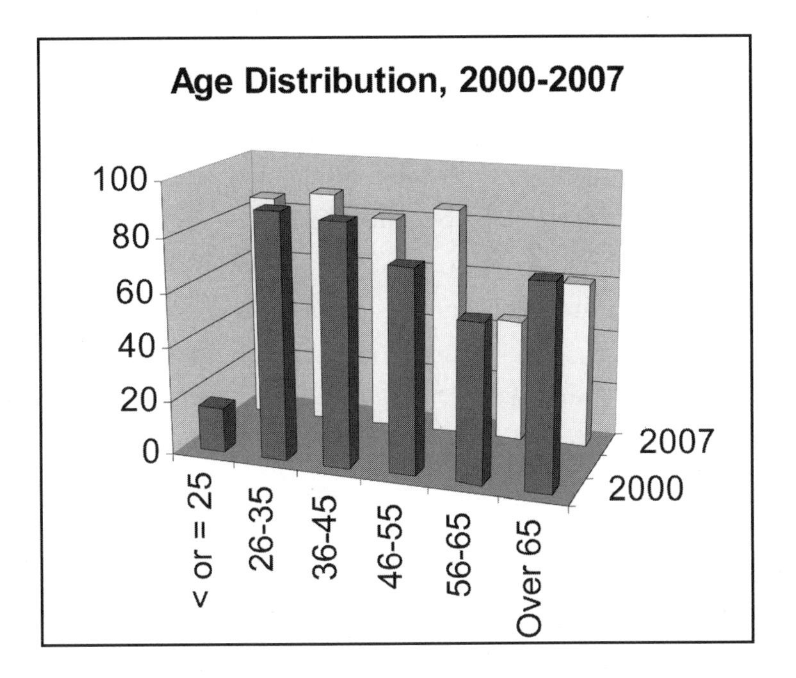

TIP: *Charts and graphics are one way to introduce color and design elements to add visual interest that will help to hold the attention of the grant reviewer.*

Another way to present evidence of need is through recounting the experiences and work of other organizations that have attempted to address this or a similar problem in the same community or elsewhere. Describe the level of success their efforts were able to achieve. Are those programs still in operation, and if not, why not? If this program's chosen approach tackles the problem in a different way, for what reason was it chosen as an alternative approach? Why is this proposed program the better or best way to solve the problem, and does it address the root causes of the problem or at least alleviate suffering when a problem is too large? For example, this would be the difference between an immunization program to prevent a disease and a program to dispense medication that might not be affordable otherwise. Similarly, it may be possible to cite the work of a known expert in the field, results of his or her research, or a well-placed quotation.

Although data can illustrate quantifiable information quickly, sometimes little data is available or it does not convey the emotional toll that the affected people may be experiencing. Award-winning grants enable grant reviewers to connect with the situation emotionally, and that requires more that a simple statement of facts. It can be highly effective to show the reader the needs to be addressed and put a "human face" on the problem by using one or two personal stories. Interspersion of particularly well-phrased quotes from program clients or staff can help enliven the narrative and make a proposal much more compelling. But tell these stories simply and directly. Show respect and empathy for those profiled, not pity. Also, be sure to maintain confidentiality when telling someone's personal story to a stranger.

In our example of Hope for New Life, the organization had no first-hand accounts to use in support of its program. It gave no indication that it had ever encountered its target audience. Its case could have been stronger had it been able to tell a story similar to this:

> *Joanne left school before she graduated to marry her boyfriend, and she discovered she was pregnant. He was already working at the auto repair shop, and she thought he would "take care of" her and her baby. The marriage fell apart, and the father of her child left town with no forwarding address. She had no car, job, or training. Neither did she trust anyone she knew to take care of her two-year-old daughter. Hope for New Life placed her in its General Education Diploma (GED) high school equivalency program and provided her with job training in its cosmetology career program. During this time she qualified for Aid for Families and Dependent Children (AFDC, often referred to as welfare) payments and a subsidized apartment. Hope For New Life provides free on-site day care in its child care training school while she is in class. When she graduates next month, Hope for New Life will assist her in securing permanent employment, continue to provide low cost child care, and if needed, allow her to acquire a vehicle donated and repaired*

by the auto-mechanics career program. Joanne will then have the tools to take care of her child and herself, graduate from public assistance and know the pride of her accomplishment.

They should not say something like this:

Joanne foolishly dropped out of school to marry her baby's daddy. The irresponsible lout took off and went into hiding....

If the targeted funder is one of the few that accepts photos or video with submitted requests, feel free to use this media if possible. Be sure to get written permission from those shown in the images or from the parents or guardians if they feature children.

When using personal accounts, only tell enough of the story to demonstrate the need or the point of the section being written. Too much information will obscure the point of the example and lessen its effectiveness. Above all, be sure the personal stories used clearly demonstrate the need for the program that is requesting the funds.

A GOOD NEEDS STATEMENT EXAMPLE (FICTIONAL)

The J. M. McCoy Health Center Application to the Victor Donald Foundation

1. Needs Statement

Meet Joanna. Joanna is 20 years old and until a few months ago lived in the Mill Quarter neighborhood with her mother. Her mother recently died at age 40 from breast cancer, which could have been averted had she received regular mammograms to diagnose the disease early. Joanna' father died of gangrene, a serious complication of diabetes five years ago. His erratic behavior and frequent absences from work, probably the result of his untreated condition, hampered his ability to hold down a "regular" job, and thus the family did not have health insurance. Like many they simply tried to get by without regular care, depending on over-the-counter remedies for relief and the hospital emergency room when any medical problem seemed to become unbearable. Joanna has been left without support while she tries to attend the local community college to get certified as a Licensed Practical Nurse. Just five months short of her goal, Joanna is struggling to cope with her mother's death, and has moved in with friends and increased her

A GOOD NEEDS STATEMENT EXAMPLE (FICTIONAL)

work hours so that she can support herself. She is still waiting to hear if she will be able to receive increased scholarship assistance in order to pay her tuition. In Mill Quarter, stories like Joanna's are heard everyday and could have been averted if families had easy access to nearby and affordable healthcare and health education.

There is a growing low income population of uninsured individuals and families in Columbia, Ohio, in particular its Mill Quarter neighborhood, and throughout the nation. The proportion of unemployed workers has increased along with an increase in the incidence of poverty in the inner-city neighborhoods. The three existing neighborhood health centers have reached their capacity and increasingly find it difficult to adequately serve everyone who appears at their doors for treatment. The Mill Quarter neighborhood is home to an increasing number of recent immigrants who are difficult to serve because of cultural and language barriers. It is the only quadrant of the city that does not have a community-based healthcare center. There are no doctors' offices or non-subsidized healthcare facilities within a three-mile radius of the proposed location of the J. M. McCoy Health Center. There is public transit available in this neighborhood, though the service to other parts of the city is limited, and many of the residents are elderly or have limited mobility. This further limits their access to proactive, primary care health services.

Columbia is in a growing region of Ohio. The city is home to the county government offices and several colleges, universities, and technical schools, including a university's school of medicine and several schools of nursing. The city hosts a professional lacrosse team, the Blues, as well as the Small Towners, a minor league baseball franchise, and numerous theater, musical, dance, and arts organizations. It is regarded as a community that is economically well diversified and buffered from extreme fluctuations of the state and regional economy.

Nonetheless, almost two-thirds of the residents of the Mill Quarter neighborhood have annual incomes of less than 80 percent the area median of $54,000. One-fourth of the residents of the neighborhood arrived in this country in the last five years and are still establishing their families and employment. An estimated 25 percent of the population is over age 65, compared to the citywide average of only 14 percent over age 65. Approximately one-third of these seniors have been unable to access Social Security or Medicare. The remaining low income residents, if working, are working in low wage, low skill positions that are often part-time, intermittent, or otherwise do not provide health insurance plans. According to a recent City Health Department

A GOOD NEEDS STATEMENT EXAMPLE (FICTIONAL)

survey, an estimated 40 percent of this neighborhood does not have access to health insurance. This creates a tremendous need for free or low cost primary care throughout the neighborhood.

The three other neighborhood health centers report steady increases in visits and can no longer schedule appointments in less than one week. This can be a critically long delay in treatment of some conditions. Even with limited transportation, residents of the Mill Quarter neighborhood accounted for 17.5 percent of neighborhood health center clientele, an increase from 12.5 percent in 2003.

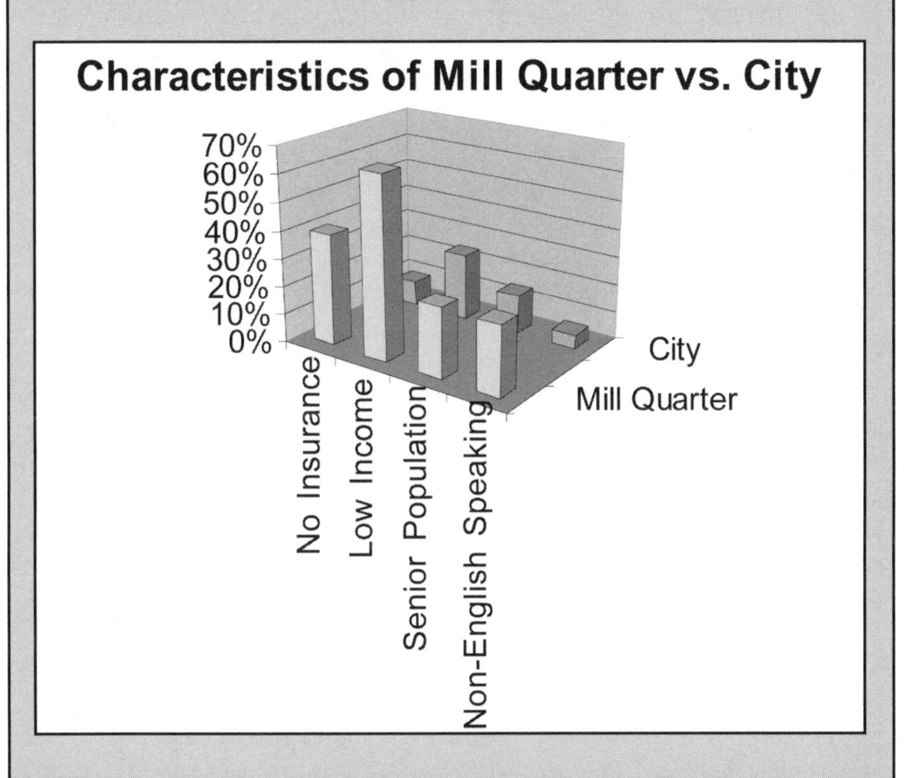

Low income populations and those with inadequate health coverage are more likely to have complications from manageable health conditions such as obesity, high blood pressure, high cholesterol, and sexually transmitted diseases. Simple primary care interventions and education from trusted healthcare providers can significantly reduce the complications of these and other conditions.

Examples of how the low income have less access to various forms of healthcare are frequently reported in the media. For example *HealthDay News* reports that

A GOOD NEEDS STATEMENT EXAMPLE (FICTIONAL)

recent studies show that only 35 percent of patients eligible for internal defibrillators received these devices after a hospitalization for heart attacks. The figure varied by ethnic groups as well, with only 28 percent of black women obtaining the devices, 29 percent of white women and 33 percent of black men, but 43 percent of white men were able to obtain this treatment. Researches hypothesized that being low income may be a contributing factor.

Another study, this one of children who "age out" of foster care with no economic support, show lowered access to health insurance and therefore healthcare, compared to the general population of their age group. "While approximately 30 percent of young adults in the general population report an episode of being uninsured over the course of the past year, we found that more than half of emancipated participants were uninsured, with rates ranging as high as 76 percent of the participants with an experience of homelessness," the researchers wrote. In addition "More than one fifth of former foster children reported an unmet need for medical care, compared to only 14 percent for youth with stable housing," the research team noted. The study appeared in the October 2007 issue of the *Archives of Pediatrics and Adolescent Medicine.*

Healthcare treatments given at the primary care level early in a disease process are shown to be as much as 50 percent less expensive than treatment by hospitalization or by emergency. Chronic diseases such as diabetes, if managed, are 47 percent less expensive than treating the severe complications that can result without medical management. In approximately 17 percent of cases, premature death can occur from unmanaged illnesses. The estimated loss of household income due to premature loss of a wage earner is estimated to be as much as $308 million each year nationally. This creates an economic, social, and emotional strain on their families.

This neighborhood, with its population of approximately 35,000 mostly low income and under- or uninsured residents easily justifies the location of a new neighborhood health center. More important, the health, welfare, and economic benefit of access to better healthcare will have direct impact on the economic and social stability of the residents and the neighborhood itself. The personal and community benefits of prevention more than outweigh the costs of providing the care.

CHAPTER SUMMARY

- Describe the problem your program intends to address.

- Quantify the size or frequency of the problem.
- Use outside sources of data to reinforce your claims.
- Summarize large amounts of data into charts or tables.
- Clearly document your sources.
- Use a few well-picked personalized accounts.
- Follow proper protocol.
- Aim to make a compelling but not overly wrought case for your request.

CHAPTER 8

WHAT WILL YOU DO? THE PROGRAM DESCRIPTION

THE FUNDER'S PERSPECTIVE

CASE STUDY: AN

AN is a design professional who serves on the review team for a local community foundation. The foundation is a large one whose primary mission is to assist donors of all sizes to direct their charitable gifts to benefit the local community. It may help individuals, families, businesses, or other foundations in making donations to like-minded foundations or with establishing their own foundations.

It helps small foundations with investment strategies for their endowments as well as with the mechanics of receiving and evaluating grant applications and with the subsequent awards and monitoring of the grantees. Along with many other types of grants, the foundation has two different grant programs to serve the arts community. One is for major arts organizations, having annual budgets of greater than $350,000, and one for small community arts organizations, having budgets of less than $350,000. It does so in the belief that both large and small arts organizations serve different but equally important roles within the community, and it provides the two-tier programs so that small groups do not have to compete with the greater expertise and recognition that the large groups have.

AN serves on the team that evaluates the smaller community arts groups applications. Although the programs now use electronic, form-based applications, the applicant must still provide narratives describing its audience and its contribution that it makes to the community through its art. When evaluating a program description, he said, "The fact that one organization might serve more people than another is not really a major criteria. We want to see that they have a

CASE STUDY: AN

definite plan for carrying out their mission. We look for groups that show that they serve a unique or important niche in the community arts spectrum. If there is no one else bringing chamber music into the schools, for example, or if not one else provides furnaces for glass blowing; if these arts might disappear but for the efforts of this group, that is a major consideration in our funding. The community arts fund does not fund groups that are so specific in activity that their sole purpose seems to be to perpetuate themselves, with no outreach and little community support or attendance. They should have a five-year strategic plan for themselves and (show with their project description) how they will serve the art and cultural needs of the community."

— AN

This chapter addresses the usual components of an award-winning program description. This material may also be presented in a section titled "Program Methodology" or "Program Activities." AN's description, above, of the focus of the grant program he reviews for demonstrates the power of a detailed program description. It provides the funder assurance that its giving mission is being met by using concrete information that is shown to relate to its funding priorities. For example, if a project aims to provide after-school child care, telling the location of the facility will show if it is in the target community, near the schools. If not, will there should be safe, reliable transportation? Otherwise, how will the children be able to access the facility? Have you described how the transportation security will be guaranteed?

In some instances the funder may request that elements of the program description be presented in other sections or separately. If so, try not to be excessively redundant between sections, but do be sure to be consistent and tie the sections together by references so that the program will be fully understood by the reader. For example, some funders will stipulate that the program description section should also include discussions of the goals and objectives of the program. They might even ask that each goal statement be followed with a listing of the specific program activities that relate directly to the accomplishment of that goal. Similarly, the instructions for the program description section may ask for a discussion of how the program might be replicated by others, proof that it is not a duplication of the efforts of others, and other key components of a complete grant application. Although this book attempts to address each of these key components in separate chapters, you will have to be ready to blend various sections as instructed by the target grant program.

The easiest way to understand how to present a program description is to use the "five Ws" guidelines used by journalists: Tell who will do what, when, where, and why. The "why" will relate directly to the needs statement. All program activities should be described in the framework of how they meet the goals of the program (more about goals in Chapter 10) and, in a larger sense, the mission of the organization. In this section the grant writer must provide enough detail for the reader to understand exactly what the service is, who will receive it, and where and how it will be delivered.

Create a step-by-step description of the policies and procedures of the program. Start with a description of the target clientele, eligibility requirements, and planned outreach and marketing efforts to secure applicants. What staff members or volunteers will provide intake and provide the actual services? Will there be open applications to, registration for, or referrals to the program? Will there be a batching of candidates, as might occur in an educational program? Or will the services be available on a continuous basis as soon as an opening is available? Describe how the service will handle greater demand than available openings. Will there be a waiting list, with the opportunity to join later, or is it expected that all applicants will be served relatively quickly after they have completed their application process?

Program descriptions can be developed for building or renovation projects also. For these, useful graphics might include maps of the location of the project, photos of the existing conditions, and perhaps sketches or plans for the proposed changes. The funder may want a detailed scope of work for the building project: how large will it be? What will be the capacity that the finished structure can serve? What is the expected life span of the finished structure? How will it function? Are there alternative ways to build the structure? If so, why was the one you propose chosen? Will professional tradesmen be required? How much of the labor or materials, if any, are being donated or obtained at a reduced price? Are there regulations (such as zoning), inspections or permits (such as building permits) to be obtained? What governing bodies need to approve the project (the local building office, a county health department, the local fire inspector, a state building commission, or maybe multiple agencies)? What impact does coordination with these have on the schedule? What are the steps for obtaining permits, inspections, and approvals? Does land or a location need to be acquired? What is the status of negotiations for a site for the construction? What will be the steps in the building or renovation project?

An individual seeking support, for example a writer applying for a residency, will describe the project concept and the ancillary activities, such as research, that will occur during the desired residency. Do you aspire to produce, for example, a historical novel, a biography, a new symphony, or a series of pottery pieces? What is the medium or materials you will use? Are you exploring a new method or working in one that is uniquely yours? What inspires your work? What research needs to be done? Does the location of this residency, workshop, or other assistance that is fixed by location, hold special advantage for accomplishing your research or your work? For example, is a special library or historic collection located nearby? Are people that you would like to interview or interact with located in the area? Describe the process you will use to create your work. For example, do you still need to develop the concept for the work, or are you ready to begin preliminary sketches or outlines? Are the sketches done and you simply need studio space and time to create the work? Is there a special place to unveil your work when completed? How will the terms of the residency, for example, teaching art classes to inner city children, help to reinforce the creative process for your own work? What other conditions are necessary for you to successfully complete the work? Will anyone own the rights to the work when completed?

This is the section that should explain how you will incorporate your unique or borrowed theories and methods into the service. If the approach is unique in some way, or even if it is not, list the factors that were key to the decision to use one method over another or possibly in conjunction with another. If partnerships with others allow cost savings by sharing overhead costs, space, or in some other way gain leverage, describe how this combined effort is more effective. Describe in detail the rights and responsibilities of each member of the partnership and generally how that relationship will operate.

Program design will also have a time component. Time may be constrained by how long the funds available would last, or a funding source may dictate that their funds awarded be spent and reported on within a given time period. Therefore, when planning a program, it is necessary to envision when it can most feasibly begin, which steps must occur before others, how much time each step will take, whether some steps can occur simultaneously, which steps are dependent on outside occurrences, and whether there are constraints related to other calendars, holidays, and the school year. The sequence of events in a program can be graphically summarized with the use of schedules or milestone charts. These have the advantage of visually linking tasks or events (milestones) to a time continuum. To be most effective the milestone chart should still be linked with a narrative explanation of these factors and tasks in the program description. Careful attention to this process may reveal to program designers certain flaws or coordination problems that can be worked out prior to starting the program. It is important to build into the schedule the evaluation steps that will be built into your process and plan for the submission of regular status reports to your benefactors. Creation of and adherence to a schedule for implementation of the grant-funded portion of a program is a vital step in future success of the program.

The program design and methodology should show a clear connection to the applicant organization's mission and the needs in its community. Discuss in the program description exactly how it promotes the organization's mission in its community and the connection to the needs. Following up on your earlier research into the grant maker, also use this section to explain or show how the program advances the objectives and interests of the grant maker. Leave no question that this is a program it will want to fund, not only because of the compelling need for the program and not only because of this superior plan for execution of the program, but because this is exactly the type of program it explicitly was formed to support.

We will continue our study of the ineffective Hope for New Life's Application, which you can contrast with the sample of an effective program description provided immediately afterward.

CASE STUDY: HOPE FOR NEW LIFE

From the hypothetical application for Community Development Block Grant funds submitted by Hope For New Life, a social service agency serving Some Town, Ohio

C. Program Description

We will begin by locating a facility for the child care center, which ideally will include space for the classroom education component and the administrative offices. The second step will be to renovate and furnish the facility. We will then open our doors and make our services known through the community with an aggressive radio and television advertising campaign. Initially the members of the board will provide the direct service and begin recruiting additional qualified staff. Adding additional positions will correspond to the number of children served in the center. Ultimately we will employ some of our graduates in our child care center.

CASE STUDY: HOPE FOR NEW LIFE

When that part is operational, we will expand to developing the car repair operation. We will try to get donations of the tools required along with the vehicles to work on. Completed cars will be donated to needy students of our training programs upon their graduation.

Analysis: The founder of Hope for New Life believed that this description was so obviously effective that the city would be thrilled to hand over a significant amount of the available $9 million. It is a start of a plan, but much more detail and thought is required to qualify for any funding. The following sample is much more effective.

EXAMPLE OF AN EFFECTIVE PROGRAM DESCRIPTION (FICTIONAL)

2. Program Description

The community food bank will be open to all members of the Mill Quarter neighborhood in Columbia, Ohio, without consideration of age, race, national origin, religion, family status, or ability to pay. Our outreach and marketing activities will rely heavily on free public announcements in the "What's Going On?" section of the neighborhood newspaper that is delivered free on Thursdays. The five local churches have agreed to place posters on their bulletin boards. The clergy have been involved in planning the program and are committed to referring individuals to the food bank who are in need of emergency assistance, in particular a three-day food supply. Also, the local welfare office and United Appeal are partnering to provide additional funding to the food bank and to distribute information about the food bank to its clients. Joe's Sign Shop is donating a lighted, attractive sign for the front of the building that will make it easy to find the facility.

Volunteers have been recruited from throughout the community, but especially from church youth groups, athletic teams, local government employees, and members of the business community. So far there is a core group of 25 to work at the food bank and establish the services. Some of the more experienced volunteers will assist in continuing recruitment of new and replacement volunteers. Particularly sought after will be volunteers that are able to speak one or more of the several languages used in the neighborhood. Eventually it is hoped that some of those who have been served by the food bank will be inspired to "give back" by volunteering themselves, within the center and by reaching out to their neighbors and friends to encourage use of the service to maintain good health and nutrition.

In-kind donations to date have included the sign mentioned above, new and used

EXAMPLE OF AN EFFECTIVE PROGRAM DESCRIPTION (FICTIONAL)

office equipment, and nonperishable food and household items. The building space is being donated by a local property owner, and church groups are assisting with cleanup and painting. Local contractors are volunteering their time to plan and supervise needed renovations to the electrical and plumbing systems. The United Appeal, the County Health Department, and All Saints Hospital are donating new computers and inventory systems, miscellaneous office supplies, and nonprescription remedies such as antibiotic creams, aspirin, and band-aids. The funds from this grant request of $10,000 are needed to pay for 50 percent of the one-year operational needs, including utility costs, insurance, telephone service, and office supplies. The remaining 50 percent has already been pledged by the Shipley Company Foundation.

The food bank includes a comfortable office for working on records; a break room for shoppers, outfitted with toys for children; a private registration booth; an administrative office; storage and display space; a shipping and receiving area; separate restrooms for the public and staff; a break area for the volunteers and staff; and a conference/meeting room for training, educational programs, and private consultations.

Nonperishable food and household supply donations are received at the loading dock from 9 a.m. till 4 p.m. Monday through Saturday, the same as our hours of operation. Volunteers help to sort and shelve the items and rotate the stock so that the older supplies are used first. Cash donations are received usually through the mail. If earmarked for direct assistance, they are used to purchase gift cards in $10 increments, which the clients can take to local supermarkets for fresh produce, meat, and dairy items.

When individuals visit the food bank they will be greeted by a multilingual volunteer who will determine the family size and give the client a basic shopping list for a three-day supply of food and a shopping cart for the visit. They will be able to search the stocked shelves and select the food items from the selection available in each category that meets their family preferences. This small amount of client control over the food selection helps to ensure that the entire supply will be used as intended and allows the client to feel less degraded and more empowered when accessing this critical assistance. Because of the high demand for food assistance, the food bank does have to restrict assistance to only one visit per month for each household served.

The facility plans to conduct nutritional education classes as well as to provide the client with access to a social service resource coordinator to assist in referrals to other agencies and support that the family may be in need of. Assistance will be

EXAMPLE OF AN EFFECTIVE PROGRAM DESCRIPTION (FICTIONAL)

available for scheduling follow-up care. If the resource coordinator determines that the client may be suffering from a neglected mental or health condition, he or she will recommend a visit to our sister medical clinic in the neighborhood to help assure that needed medications are available. Clients will be linked to partner organizations providing assistance with obtaining other needs, such as rent assistance or utility payments.

The Executive Director is responsible for supervising the efficient operation of the food bank and for organizing community outreach activities. Outreach is needed to not only ensure that prospective clients are aware the help is available when they need it, but also to raise awareness of hunger in the community and develop ongoing donations and support for the food bank.

In the program summary and in the budget, if it is presented as a separate section, the applicant will state the amount of the request, as well as the proportion of the total project costs and revenues this request represents. In the program description tell the funder exactly how the funds will be used, whether for activities, materials, equipment, staff, or some other portion of the entire program. This section should explain briefly how the organization intends to raise the rest of the money or other resources needed to complete the project. Explain any qualifications, certifications, or licenses that need to be acquired, whether for the facility, staff, or the organization itself. Have those credentials been acquired already, or is there a plan to put them into place in the near future? Perhaps portions of the service are being provided by, or coordinated with, another organization or with volunteers. If so, introduce that organization, or the volunteer group, its experience, training, strengths, and the procedures and controls that will be used to ensure an efficient and effective collaboration.

Using collaborations might be an outgrowth of the analysis of whether the program is a duplication of effort. If not requested as a separate section, the program description would include a discussion of whether the program duplicates similar services or is unique and perhaps can be replicated (see Chapter 9).

CHAPTER SUMMARY

- Tell the "five Ws":
    - Who, what, when, where, why
- Describe special training and licenses needed.
- Show how the program answers the identified need.
- Relate the program's impact to the organization's mission.
- Relate the program's impact to the funder's interests and mission.
- Describe step-by-step how the program will be carried out.
- Provide a schedule or milestone chart.
- Describe collaborative efforts.

CHAPTER 9

IS THE PROGRAM DUPLICATED EFFORT OR EASILY REPLICATED?

CASE STUDY: DIANNE HARRIS

When a the board of a local merchants' association heard about a grant opportunity that would provide funds to improve the exterior appearance of buildings and businesses in its historic downtown, it was very excited. One potential drawback was that its local government was the only eligible grantee.

The municipality would also be required to establish an architectural review process and match the funds with capital projects in the downtown district. A quick meeting with council members, many of them business owners themselves, showed they were reluctant to impose new restrictions on the businesses that would not benefit directly from the grant activities, not to mention the need to reprioritize capital improvement projects to meet the requirements of this grant. A few skeptics believed that the program would not be used and be a waste of effort.

I was able to help the merchants' association identify a source of funds that was smaller, perhaps only enough to do one or two buildings in the district, and would not place the additional obligations on the municipality which worried the council. We found two business owners that were definitely interested in participating, and our demonstration project was born. We replicated the processes used by another community group. We obtained the lesser funds, renovated the business façades, and generated a lot of interest, not only from the other businesses in the district but from shoppers, all of whom were excited to see the impact on the appearance of the district from just these two businesses. When they found out it was a grant,

CASE STUDY: DIANNE HARRIS

many businesses began lobbying the council for more funding. Having set up and experimented with the implementation of the program, we were able to demonstrate in the application for the larger grant that we had the need and the interest for the project. We were able to show that our initial success with the program prepared us to replicate the project on a larger scale.

Analysis: The grant guidelines may ask for narratives to answer these questions: "Is the program a duplication of effort?" or "Can the program be replicated elsewhere?" In the case described above, the merchants' association was able to use the demonstration concept to overcome objections from a needed partner in a bigger project. It was able to replicate the actions of similar communities in the state. The funding agency in this case found the demonstration and replication to be desirable features. There were successes in other communities using the same approach. However, had there been another grant source available to the community that provided the same assistance and had plenty of available funds, the funder might have been disinclined to fund our group in favor of a community with no other resources.

Even if the applicant is not specifically asked to provide duplication and replication information, it is effective to at least discuss the issue in either the needs statement, as seen in Chapter 7, or the program description, as seen in Chapter 8. Note the difference in the two analysis questions above. These are not two ways of asking the same question, and the answers are also not mutually exclusive. As the case above demonstrates, there is not necessarily a right answer to either for every funder. Some funders, depending on their priorities, do have a preference to one or both questions. One may have a preference for funding a truly unique project or approach, as in the demonstration or innovation purpose grant. It may have a preference for creating information and processes that are easily adapted for use in many other communities, enabling cost savings for those that adopt the system you have created with its funding. Others may want to ensure that programs having similar clientele and focus are not unnecessarily competing for clients, funding and community support, preferring to establish complementary services instead. Information about the grantor's preferences may be expressly stated in its guidelines or funding priorities that you learn when you research the funder. Other times its preference must be deduced from the provided information about the foundation's goals and objectives in providing grants. More detail about analyzing these questions follow in this chapter.

The case above also demonstrates some of the reasons it is important to interact with and partner with peers at other charities and not-for-profit organizations. Networking allows you to borrow and share ideas for successful implementation of a new or expanded program. It allows you to understand the network of programs and services that are already being provided in the community and to get ideas about how to overcome obstacles to your objectives. Even though an organization may be addressing the same problem in your locale, you may have noticed that there are too few available resources to match the level of need, or new approaches or technologies may have developed that can be applied in a new, more effective approach to solving a problem. It is necessary to fully understand the proposed program's niche in, and relationship to, the existing service network. Armed with this understanding it is possible to put forth convincing arguments as to whether the proposal idea is a duplication and why or why not. If it is you must provide specific data and information, not just broad, generalized, and unsubstantiated statements, to prove that additional funding for your project is a good idea. About replication, show how this community is in a unique situation, or not, and what barriers might need to be overcome in order for another organization in another community to adopt the proposed program to address similar needs. Where replication is desirable funders may even ask that you will help to share your experiences with others as a condition of a grant award.

IS THE PROGRAM A DUPLICATED EFFORT?

Some foundations do not like to fund exactly duplicated efforts, targeted toward the same clientele, especially if there appears to be adequate existing funding. They do not want to pay to set up a program that may not be of any interest or importance to the client group. They also do not want to be competing for community donations and financial support to fund the same services that other not-for-profits are operating. If others are engaged in a similar activity, be sure to document clearly in your proposal narrative why your program or approach is different enough to warrant further attention.

Perhaps it is that the need for the service is far greater than the level of the currently available service. Are the sheer numbers of those in need demonstrably larger than the number that the current system can serve? Are there long waiting lists for currently available services? Perhaps the problem is location; is it necessary to physically locate closer to a particular neighborhood or client group because of transportation problems? Is there a need for the same service within a different target population? For example, perhaps career services are targeted at single mothers only, and the new program will reach out to single, unemployed fathers. In addition to the narratives, use data tables, citation of research findings, and original information from other leaders about area waiting lists, "turn away" rates, success rates, or shortages to document gaps or under-served niches in the service system.

DEMONSTRATION PROJECTS, OR CAN IT BE REPLICATED ELSEWHERE?

Perhaps the project is something new. If so, does it address an emerging need that other communities may be experiencing? Some funders are interested in disseminating new ideas to other organizations. If so, they may ask for descriptions of how a similar program could be replicated by others to address the same unmet need in other locations. In this situation, take extra time to describe in detail how the program will be implemented and any prerequisite activities or resources that need to be developed to set the stage for the program.

Likewise, if the needs to be addressed are unique to an area, show how and why they are unique. Why might the program be more difficult to replicate? Somewhat unique situations include the impact of the loss of a major employer or industry, particularly resource-based industries, or a natural disaster that affects a large portion of the community. Even in such situations, there may be parallels to other situations, and this program may provide a framework for someone else to use in structuring a similar but unique program.

Perhaps a program is a new startup but on a small scale and the intention is to test the effectiveness of the approach, or maybe there is a need to gather and analyze data to support more expensive or complex future programs. This type of program would be presented as a "demonstration" program. Demonstration programs serve as "living laboratories" in which new processes or approaches to emerging problems can be tested. It may be possible to provide proof that an approach is cost effective, to determine whether there may be measurable secondary benefits, or otherwise to produce information that would encourage others to try this program again. Some funders that like to promote innovation may seek out demonstration programs. However, some prefer to support projects that are known to be effective to maximize the benefit created by their investments.

Assuming the results are positive, other communities and organizations will be able to learn from the program and perhaps implement their own project more quickly and efficiently. Some funders have priorities for disseminating workable solutions and information to others. By funding a program that can be easily replicated, the funder is assured that its investment will multiply itself, having a greater impact, when the "ramp up" period or costs for other organizations can be reduced. Because of this, it is easy to see that the keeping of detailed data about costs and outcomes can be useful to peer organizations. Chapter 16 further discusses post-grant record-keeping and reporting. Keep in mind, though, that when a program can be replicated, it will generally enhance how a proposal is reviewed and the organization's effectiveness in winning grant awards. To continue our study of Hope for New Life, do not address this issue as it would have:

CASE STUDY: HOPE FOR NEW LIFE

From the hypothetical application for Community Development Block Grant funds submitted by Hope For New Life, a social service agency serving Some Town, Ohio

CLASSIFIED CASE STUDIES™ directly from the experts

D. Duplication of Effort Section

Our program is unique with its one-stop accessibility and multidisciplinary approach. It is obvious that the state agency and its partner nonprofits are not being effective because the incidence of poverty continues to climb. We represent a unique new approach that we hope to license and sell to other communities once we demonstrate our effectiveness. That will produce an additional income stream to support our operations.

Analysis: Hope for New Life misses the mark again, as several other agencies in the town attempt similar multidisciplinary approaches, but the organizers made assumptions that they did not research. An experienced local reviewer would recognize this misinformation immediately. Also, the intent to license the approach for gain does not match the city funding agency's goal of replicating successful projects in order to save money on administrative costs for future grantees.

CHAPTER SUMMARY

- Network with and research other organizations and programs.
- Avoid exactly duplicating existing programs in the area.
    - Increasing the amount of service or changing focus is acceptable
- Clearly show the need for a program and why it is not an unsupportable duplication.

- Show how the program can be replicated in other areas.
  - Prerequisites
  - Thorough description of preparation and implementation steps
- Be sure to address these issues in the narrative if the funder specifically requests it.

CHAPTER 10

HAVE MEASURABLE GOALS & OBJECTIVES

CASE STUDY: HOPE FOR NEW LIFE

The organizers of Hope for New Life, introduced in Chapter 1, having no understanding of the magnitude of the enterprises they intended to undertake, had no goals for the outcomes of their work.

They thought they could decide how "far" the sum of money they sought would take them after they went "shopping" for staff, space, licenses, and all the many expenses their enterprises would entail. To a potential reviewer their only goal seemed to be to get a hold of more than $9 million and cut out a tidy administration fee for themselves. Their goals section would be very short, perhaps as follows.

From the hypothetical application for Community Development Block Grant funds submitted by Hope For New Life,
a social service agency serving Some Town, Ohio

D. Goals and Objectives

Our objective is to end poverty in our community. We will train as many people as we can with the amount of funding you award us.

Analysis: So is that one, two, or three people served for $9 million? Read on for a much better example.

MORE EFFECTIVE APPROACH TO GOALS

CASE STUDY: DIANNE HARRIS

In the sample application presented in the Appendix for a microbusiness program (which is based on a real-life case), the community development department had set a goal for itself of providing tuition to an entrepreneur program at the local technical college for at least ten hopeful businesspeople and to provide startup loans for five of those that could be expected to actually proceed to the next step of starting a business.

All training and startup loans were to be completed within 12 months of project funding. These goals were established according to need and interest expressed by a community survey, were related to funding available, and had a definite time limitation. The grant reviewers understood the criteria for which the agency's performance could be evaluated and exactly how much benefit could be expected for a specific investment amount.

— Dianne Harris

How is the term "goal" defined? It has been said that a goal is a dream with a time limit. A goal has the dimension of being directly drawn from the "dream," or vision, and mission of the organization. This chapter will address how to develop your goals and objectives and how to set up an evaluation system, including defining the units of service you deliver. Your program methodology (presented in the program design section) and your budget must be designed so that they enable you to meet your objectives. The budget and degree to which you attract users for your service will dictate the numerical goal of units of service you will deliver.

By this point, the need and a specific course of action have been completely and thoroughly described, but there must also be one or more measurable goals for the program and for the use of the grant funds requested. The objectives of the program will be a broad, overreaching set of desired results. Goals are often referred to as a sort of map that shows what the final destination is. You would not set out on a major trip without a map or directions, and every project needs goals. Goals will help to focus the organization's efforts and to establish a practical relationship between the amount of funding that can be raised and the amount of impact the program can have.

Sometimes the term "goals" is used interchangeably with the term "objectives." For the purposes of this book, end results that have dimensions of quantity and time will be called measurable goals, or just goals. The goal for a particular program may not be to completely eliminate a specific problem, but an achievable goal might be to make a difference for a certain number of people for a certain time period. For example, a daily meal home-delivery program will not eliminate world hunger. However, maybe it can ensure that 200 elderly people in the community are adequately nourished through at least one meal a day within a single year.

Programs will have outcomes that are indirect, difficult to measure, or that address more than one need of the targeted clientele. For example, a meal delivery service to the elderly might also ensure that a lonely person has someone to talk to every day and thus help to alleviate loneliness and depression. It may also provide, through the delivery person, someone who could detect an emergency situation and call for help. Thus, there could be multiple benefits from a single seemingly straightforward activity of delivering one meal a day.

When outcomes from a program may seem to be unmeasurable, such as "increasing the self-esteem of girls aged 10 to 13 from single-parent homes," it may be necessary to measure an associated indicator to demonstrate the attainment of goals. For example, can the program count the number of girls in that age group that participated? How long did they participate? Is it possible to have the participants complete questionnaires that rate levels of attitudes or behaviors that are related to self-esteem at the beginning and at the end of the program? Do their grades improve after the program, as an indicator of self-esteem? Do destructive behaviors decrease? So, for example, a goal might be to find increases in grade-point averages by one half letter grade for at least 50 percent of participants. Or it might be to observe a 25 percent decrease in the rate of smoking, as indicators of increased self-esteem.

This is what we mean by defining your units of service to measure. Organizations that provide more than one service may want to track each service type individually, for example, how many vaccinations are given and how many prescriptions are delivered. But they may be asked to also provide a count of how many households or individuals are served "without duplication." For example a single person might receive more than one vaccination and more than one prescription medication, for a total service unit count of two or more. However, this is still only one person.

Organizations that serve the homeless often are required to not only count the number of beds and number of nights of occupancy, but to provide a count by household served. An individual using the facility might receive seven nights of housing until better arrangements can be found but is only one household. A family of three might receive the same seven nights but use three beds each night, for a total occupancy count of 21, or three individuals but only one family. It can be helpful to find out how your funding agency wants to measure certain services, so that your record-keeping will easily provide the information you are going to need.

Individuals must still consider how to define their goals and objectives for their efforts. A writer may not want to have a goal of publishing a novel; after all, it may not be accepted right away. But it would be reasonable to say that an outline and first three chapters will be completed within a six-week period, for example. Longer residencies or sabbaticals, for example of nine months to a year, might lead to the submission of the novel to a publisher and three related articles to business journals. A musician might produce an album of 12 original compositions in a given length of time, or a mural painter may be able to design and paint one 40-foot tall by 60-foot wide painting on the side of a prominent building in a year.

Some funders require only that you show them how you intend to measure a program's effects. If they do not stipulate, you will have to develop a methodology for measuring a project's outcomes. Describe to the funder how the program will conduct the measurements and how often. Measurement methodologies begin with good record-keeping and accounting. Record how many volunteers or staff deliver X number of units of the service each day, each week, or each month. That will reveal, for example, how many meals are actually delivered each day, week, and month. Records of past performance are good indicators of expected future participation if such data exists. Nothing is more frustrating than to work with an applicant that wants more money but cannot tell, when asked, exactly how many people it has served in the past. Even worse is when the applicant becomes defensive and offended that a funder would dare ask the organization to spend time on activities not directly related to "helping."

If you are struggling with how to define your objectives and goals, revisit the original concept for the program. Review the need you are addressing. Why did you choose the process that you will use to solve that problem? What are your priorities? A given clientele may have multiple needs, and you may desire ultimately to address all of them. But in general you can effectively take on only three to five new activities at a time, depending on your organization's size. Brainstorming with trusted friends, your board of advisors, or even alone is a good next step. Generate a simple list of all the objectives you could be addressing. Look at the available or potential resources you have, whether in personnel, volunteers, funds, and facility assets. Which of these position you for quick implementation of a few of these objectives? Which objectives are feasible in the grant period of the funds you are seeking? This should reduce your list.

From this reduced list, do a simple comparison exercise in which you compare only two of these options at a time. This process imitates the binary decision process that computers do. Ask yourself, and your panel, if used, the following question: Should work begin on X activity before work begins on Y activity? The choice of X or Y will depend on many tangible and intangibles that affect your current situation. When the choice has been made, order them on an imaginary schedule. Most people would by convention place the chosen "first" item to the left. Then select another item and ask the same question, comparing it to the first choice of the last comparison: Should work begin on Z activity before work begins on X? If yes, move Z to the appropriate location. If the answer is no, compare Z to Y. Then position it between X and Y or after Y, as indicated. Continue to sort through your options. Select the top three to five, depending on how large those efforts seem to be, as your priority activities. These are your program objectives.

To then determine your measurable goals, do the following. Consider each priority activity and generate a time-ordered list of sub-events or activities that must occur under each activity. Based on the cost per unit to complete that activity and time needed for each activity, you will create your action plan. You can now make a correspondence between how much of each service or activity you can reasonably be able to achieve with the grant funding you are seeking in the time period you will have it available. Break these into as many distinct activities as seems reasonable, and you have created your measurable goals. For example, a healthcare service may have an objective to increase the health status of the community. But it determines that to have this effect, it must conduct certain standard healthcare procedures, such as, conduct a health history on every patient who visits, every time he or she visits: this equals X health histories. The number of vaccinations, prescriptions for medication, stitches for lacerations, referrals to other organizations, or any and all of the many medical procedures that the agency might provide are all estimated separately (perhaps using some statistical probability) and equals the Y number of procedures. The number of individuals and households represents A and B goals that can be distinctly measured and reported.

EXAMPLE GOALS, OBJECTIVES, & EVALUATION PLAN (FICTIONAL)

J. M. McCoy Health Center, Continued

3. Program Mission, Goals, and Objectives

The mission of the J. M. McCoy Health Center is to improve the lives of the residents of the Mill Quarter neighborhood through better health, healthy habits, and increased connection with the wider community.

The goals for having a community health center in this location are:

a. To make primary healthcare more accessible to those with limited ability to pay, limited transportation, or language barriers

b. To reduce usage of emergency room facilities for non-emergency healthcare

c. To reduce the incidence of serious medical problems that result from progression of unattended medical needs

d. To use health education to improve health habits and reduce the incidence of serious medical problems

Some of these goals are more long-term effects of the immediate activity of delivering primary healthcare and education. But they are effects that will have long-term major benefits to improve lives of low income families. By helping them remain healthier, they will have fewer missed work or school days. They will have reduced stress if work and income are more stable. Education of the young will be enhanced if attendance is better, which will increase chances for better employment and security in their future. Overall medical costs of treating serious medical conditions will be reduced if simpler interventions are taken before those conditions arise. Medical costs can be reduced over the entire healthcare system if those having little access to primary care are given an affordable alternative to emergency rooms for non-emergency care.

The center plans to start modestly, to use available resources to their maximum benefit, and slowly grow the program as outreach efforts are more successful and demonstrable success attracts more volunteers and funding.

EXAMPLE GOALS, OBJECTIVES, & EVALUATION PLAN (FICTIONAL)

To that end, the first year's measurable objectives include:

a. To provide primary treatment to 30 patients per day, 5.5 days per week, a total of 8,580 visits per year

b. To provide group health education classes to 10 persons per class, holding 2 classes per month, for a total of 240 attendees per year. Some individuals may avail themselves of more than one class per year.

c. To achieve an increase of childhood immunizations — such that all neighborhood children will be up to date on their immunization schedule by the end of the year

d. To reduce the number of non-emergency visits by Mill Quarter neighborhood residents to the All Saints Hospital emergency room by 2,000 per year (from the current 4,000 per year as tracked by zip code of patient

4. Monitoring and Evaluation

The service will be evaluated and monitored through several mechanisms. First of all, volunteers will assist in the gathering of statistics on usage both daily and compiled. Specific services will be tabulated, such as:

- Children immunized at the center
- Patients screened and/or treated for diabetes and high blood pressure
- Referrals to more advanced care
- Flu shots given
- Number served who do not speak English
- Number assisted in smoking cessation and smoke-free three months later

Along with follow-up care, visitors will be asked to mail back comment cards that may be filled out anonymously regarding their satisfaction with the service and their treatment. There will also be quarterly surveys of the partnering organizations to solicit feedback on their observations of the success of the program based on the experiences of their clientele. The results of surveys and comment cards will be presented in board and staff/volunteer meetings for consideration and discussion as to whether aspects of the service should be adjusted to provide better client confidence and more effective communication and treatment.

CHAPTER SUMMARY

- Goals are the map showing the destination.
- A funder deserves to know how much good their investment will be accomplishing.
    - Groups often have to report this information to their donors.
- Establish a reasonable set of goals that can be accomplished in the time constraints of the grant.
- Establish a reasonable set of goals that can be accomplished in the constraints of the budget.
- Describe secondary or multiple benefits achieved from an activity.
- Evaluation is how a program's impact is measured against established goals.
- Develop a methodology to measure outcomes and success in reaching goals.
- Keep necessary records.
- Describe record-keeping and outcome measurement procedures.
    - Once it has been outlined in the grant application, the procedure is ready to implement when funds arrive.

CHAPTER 11

THE BUDGET & HOW MUCH TO ASK FOR

THE FUNDER'S PERSPECTIVE, CONTINUED

CASE STUDY: AN

"The foundation (introduced by AN in Chapter 4) will not invest in an arts group that is financially unstable or has no plan for meeting or controlling its expenses into the future. For example, we have one group that we support, that even though it carries some debt for major equipment and has significant income from classes and service fees, it still has a small gap between expenses and revenues.

"More important from our perspective, however, it is implementing a sound financial plan for paying down its debt. In contrast, another group that we have supported in the past recently lost its coordinator, and it is unclear whether adequate financial processes and controls exist to ensure that this will remain a wise investment. Its mission is very important to the community, so we struggled to find a way to continue its funding but to protect the confidence of our donors. We are as a result negotiating a phased payout process with them. In this way, we can help to control the flow of funds on a performance basis to ensure that their administrative capacity rebounds to its previous level."

— AN

As AN's examples show, the funder has a genuine interest in its beneficiaries' success. The budget is an important tool for not only justifying the amount of the funding request, but also for demonstrating financial stability and responsibility. This is why many funders of large awards sometimes also request that the applicant submit as many as three recent years' financial statements, often with a requirement that these statements have been audited by an outside party. In this way the funder can review the applicant's financial trends and verify that the requested funds are a reasonable amount.

A budget consists of two primary components, the cost of the activity side (or expenses) and the funds available and expected. The budget section will request, at a minimum, a statement of the cost of delivering the service or cost of equipment purchased plus installation, contrasted with the gap in funds available to contribute to this purpose. Most will also ask for some documentation of the costs you present. These may be written quotations, catalog listings, or certified cost estimates from professionals, such as appraisers or engineers. Some grants will require a presentation of the organization's entire annual budget or an annual report listing all assets and liabilities, with details about the specific uses of the requested grant funds. These grantors believe such information is needed to fully understand the applicant's status and skills. It is in a sense a form of underwriting to help them choose which causes to support. AN's cases also suggest the importance of the qualifications of key staff people, as detailed later in Chapter 12.

HOW MUCH IS AVAILABLE?

Grant catalogs will often show the typical size of grants made by the organization, as well as minimum and maximum award restrictions, if any. This information is sometimes missing from guidelines you might obtain directly from charitable foundations, so it is worthwhile to double-check the catalogs in addition to material available directly from the funder. If a funder makes awards significantly larger than what is needed for the proposed project, it is not wise to inflate a program's scope in an effort to make it "fit." However, if its awards are smaller, it is worth approaching more than one funder to piece together enough funds needed to complete a project.

If a project can be clearly broken down into components, it may be possible to find grant funding for one or more specific pieces. For example, Nike Corporation, through its Bowerman Track Program, provides recycled crumb rubber to install as a resilient surface on walking or running tracks. Other funds or donations can be sought out for the installation costs. Silicon Valley companies are known to provide computers or components to needy schools and libraries. Although it may seem "simpler" to apply for only one "big" grant, that one big grant may not exist for the project. The grant seeker must be flexible and creative in searching available resources and should be willing to do the work (see Chapters 2-3). After all, free money is free money. Besides, it is all right to reuse your own narratives and information in proposals to several different foundations (do not plagiarize others' work, however). Once the information has been gathered and organized, it can be easier to produce another grant application for the same cause to a different funding source. Thus the return in exchange for the up-front work can yield multiple awards and is considerable, enabling an organization to expand its influence without incurring debt or overusing direct appeals.

Most of all, do not be greedy. Feel free to ask for what is needed, according to the budgeted amount, to up the program and make it viable. It is highly unlikely that a foundation would place its entire available allocation into one project, unless it was of unusual importance. An outrageously high request may be automatically thrown out without further consideration and without giving the organization an opportunity to revise the request or budget. Worse, if a proposal has been denied funding for such an impracticality, or lack of concern for others, the organization may not receive any future consideration from the grant makers.

CASE STUDY: HOPE FOR NEW LIFE

When the Hope For New Life gentleman first contacted me, he had not gathered cost estimates, had no budget formulated, and he was somewhat irritated that I was making such a big deal asking for such "trivia." He believed that the most practical approach was to prepare budgets after the organizers found out how much money they would be receiving.

Likewise, of course, they had no idea how many people they would be able to serve until they had their millions in funding in place. They offered my firm the "opportunity" to prepare their grant application on an initially pro-bono basis in exchange for a significant amount of paid work once the millions in grant dollars were received. As mentioned in the first chapter, he had been encouraged by the warm reception of his ideas by one of our city council members, who had told him to bring in a well-drafted proposal, and he could have the city's entire Community Development Block Grant (CDBG) allocation for that year. So that's what he wanted, the entire $9 million.

— Dianne Harris

The gentleman from Hope for New Life was under the impression that a funder would make an award and determine the amount of an award to a program based on how much it might like it. He then thought that he would take this amount "shopping" for whatever he wanted. This was and is totally incorrect. All the advance planning this book has recommended so far must indeed happen before approaching a funder. Once the program, its size, and material and staffing needs are determined, it is up to the applicant to obtain a reasonable estimate of the costs of all these components.

How much can or should be requested? The gap between available resources and the cost of an achievable program is the amount that should be requested in the grant application. Grants that use printed application packages and forms are explicit about wanting to contribute only enough to eliminate the gap in funding issue. Their forms will request the applicant to divulge the available resources and the cost of the program and instruct how to make the calculation of the maximum grant request that can be made, as applies in matching formulas. This chapter presents the process of obtaining estimates; valuing other resources, such as volunteers and in-kind donations; and the presentation of this information to show the amount needed to be raised from grant sources. Divulging funds generated by fund-raising activities, such as those shown in Chapter 2, serves as a part of the budget section, in addition to demonstrating community support.

The budget component of your proposal includes a cost/expense tabulation and a revenue/resources tabulation. The budget is especially adaptable for presentation in a table format. There are different approaches for tabulating all sources of funds and all uses of funds, mostly whether the table shows a summary of budget items, a detailed line-item format of budget items, or combines the sources and uses into the same table. The funder may stipulate which type or types of tables it prefers. If not, choose the format that you believe most clearly represents your request.

> **TIPS:** *Be sure that everything adds up correctly. Don't be greedy. Don't invent additional work or expenses just because you sense funds might be available. Whether an individual or an organization, your budget should not detail every paperclip needed, but it should include at least the usual major expense items, such as:*

- Salaries (including benefits)
- Rent and utilities
- Office supplies
- Printing and postage
- Materials (such as books, sports equipment, and art supplies)
- Contractual services (such as legal, audit costs, and accounting)
- Paid notices, advertising, and publicity
- Training and travel costs

A copy of the sample budget form is also included on the CD-ROM in Microsoft Word format.

TIP: *Tables created in Word can perform simple calculations.*

A SAMPLE PROGRAM BUDGET FORM SHOWING SOURCES AND USES FORMAT			
Source of Funds	Source Amount	Use of Funds	Cost
Corporate and private donations	$50,000	Salaries (including benefits) 2 @ $40,000 ea	$80,000
ABC Foundation (this application)	$41,800	Rent and utilities $700/month for 1 year	$8,400
Proceeds from spring flower sale fund-raiser	$5,000	Office supplies and postage	$1,200
In-kind donations (printing and advertising)	$ 1,000	Printing	$600
		Program materials	$1,200
		Contractual services	$2,000
		Notices and advertising	$400
		Travel and training 2 @ $2,000 ea	$4,000
Total	$97,800.00		$97,800

Be sure to annotate the sources for any cost estimates used that are derived from reference materials.

OBTAINING COST ESTIMATES

Sometimes expense items listed in the budget require obtaining written documentation from a "primary" source. The sources of information regarding the costs of your project will vary according to the type of project being proposed. Here are some ideas for simple ways to obtain this information:

Vendors: If there are furnishings, supplies, or equipment needed to operate the project, it may be simple to plan out the space — how many desks, chairs, file cabinets, computers, and such are needed — and find costs in office supply catalogs. Even with a catalog, it is worth contacting a sales representative in person. A phone call or meeting often reveals that a discount is available when purchasing multiple items. Online shopping sources can be another easy source of cost estimates for thousands of items.

Experience: If the organization is already in operation and uses similar supplies or equipment, a quick look through the last year's expenditures can yield reliable cost estimates. Be sure to make an allowance for annual inflation or salary increases.

Human Resources: The human resources department can provide the salaries of personnel in these or similar positions, as well as benefits. These may also need to be prorated if a staff person is being shared by more than one program. If there are no previously hired staff, approximations of these costs can be found from local staffing agencies or online salary surveys (see the Economic Research Institute at **www.eri-nonprofit-salaries.com**).

Peer Groups: Discretely ask peers, contacts, and mentors what they budget for staff or contracted services of a similar type.

Contractors: Those in the building trades, such as architects, contractors, and developers, have "rules of thumb," manuals, and even computer software for quickly estimating building and renovation projects, expressed as a cost per square foot. These are sometimes tiered according to the quality or level of luxury sought by the user. This accounts for the difference between the use of, for example, vinyl tile, carpet, or marble flooring. If possible, to obtain the best cost estimate and put the project out to bid, contingent on funding, prior to preparing the grant request.

Showing Staff Costs: Another note about staffing costs: The budget should show staff costs in terms of "full time equivalents," or FTEs, to avoid confusion. A staffer who works 40 hours per week is considered 1 FTE. A staffer working only 20 hours per week is considered 0.5 FTE, for example. Fringe benefits, such as company-paid insurance or paid vacation time, will be displayed as a line item separate from salaries in a detailed budget but under the more general heading of staff costs in a budget summary. The annual costs of fringe benefits should also be prorated based on whether the individual is 0.25 FTE (10 hours per week), 0.5 FTE, or 1 FTE.

Valuing In-kind and Volunteer Resources: The budget should place a reasonable value on volunteer time and services, as well as accounting for the value of any donated materials, rents, or services. If these had to be purchased, they would definitely represent a cost to the program. Funders want to see that these resources are available and that a reasonable value is allocated to them. Sometimes a funder will stipulate a standard dollar value for each hour of volunteer time to be sure that all applicants are evaluated fairly when volunteer time accounts for some of the required matching funds.

Prorated: If costs such as utilities, phone service, rent, or administrative services are to be shared with other offices or programs, the costs of these items can be prorated across all users. This is sometimes done on a percentage of the total square feet or time used by each service (this can be especially applicable for utilities and rent) or can just be divided evenly by all (more appropriate for basic phone charges). Again, existing data provides the basis for making this calculation, and the application guidelines may provide a unified system for all applicants to use.

Direct Costs and Indirect Costs: Some grants will fund only "direct costs," which are costs that are solely and directly attributable to the provision of the particular program or activity that is the subject of the grant request. For example, in the case of an organization that seeks to add an activity needing grant funding but does not need to add any staff time to implement the project, staff time is not a direct cost of the activity, though additional supplies would be. Indirect costs are general overhead and administration costs that could be attributable to several or all activities of the organization. Indirect costs are calculated by a prorated method as mentioned above. Some grants, especially government grants, forbid or discourage the funding of indirect costs. If allowed, the guidelines outline the criteria for determining the proportion of the funds that are attributable and thus fundable for the project. Government grants require such extensive documentation of indirect costs that most small grantees find other ways to cover the costs and use the direct cost methodology exclusively for administrative costs. In the case of a staff person, this is most easily done by keeping detailed time sheets that show the time spent on grant activities, charging only the total of the hourly pay rate and attributable fringe benefit costs times the number of hours to the grant.

MATCHING FUNDS

Some grant funders require that there be evidence that their contributions will be matched by cash or donated goods and services. This is an area in which it is important to accurately track the amount of volunteer time and in-kind donations received and assign appropriate values to them. See the previous discussion of Volunteer and In-kind Donations. In other cases, only a cash match will meet the requirement. When a cash match is required, it is critical to be able to show you have available uncommitted funds raised through other efforts or future potential sources of program income, as outlined in Chapter 2. These will show up as available resources on the budget summary form. Documentation of this information may include a financial statement from your accountant as well as the organization budget.

PRESENTING THE BUDGET

Although the budget lends itself to presentation in tables, a narrative description is sometimes desired or even required. It may be necessary to explain any assumptions, such as whether fringes are actually calculated amounts or percentage estimates. What is the value assigned to volunteer time, and why is that an appropriate amount? If a multi-year project, did you include cost of living increases, or inflationary factors for supplies and other expenses?

If the funder you approach does not provide forms and instructions, this chapter provides sample tables that can be used to quickly organize budget information. Determine and provide the level of budget information the funder wishes to obtain, whether a budget summary or a detailed budget is requested. Sometimes only a brief budget narrative is required, but sometimes table and narrative presentations are to be made a part of the application. A budget summary table will show broad categories of expenses and revenues. A budget detail table will show individual line items under each category. Sometimes a detailed budget will be requested. At other times, funders that prefer shorter submissions may need only the budget summary.

The sample budget summary reproduced from the J. M. McCoy Health Center application at the end of the chapter shows the proper format for presenting the total costs of the project under the "Use of Funds" columns and the "Source of Funds," those resources that are either already available or are being requested in the grant application. The requested funds are clearly pointed out with the notation "this application."

The following example of a small museum's budget summary is ineffective because of its omission of important information.

MUSEUM REQUEST X			
Source of Funds	Source Amount	Use of Funds	Cost
This Request	$10,000	Manager Salary and Fringes	$50,000
Gift Shop Proceeds	$10,000	Maintenance and Utilities	$15,000
Volunteer Time	$10,000	Run Gift Shop	$0
		Gift Shop Inventory	$2,500
Total Resources	$30,000	Total Expenses	$67,500

The above example is lacking because it does not show a balanced budget. There is no indication of how the gap between resources and expenses will be bridged. A funder will not invest in a program that is certain to fail financially. This museum project could strengthen its application by simply indicating what other sources of funds will be attempted in the interim, even if those are not realized at the time of submission. For example, there might be additional lines as follows:

MUSEUM REQUEST Y				
Source of Funds	Source Amount		Use of Funds	Cost
This Request	$10,000		Manager Salary and Fringes	$50,000
Arts Council Grant	$22,500 *	Pending	Maintenance and Utilities	$15,000
Gift Shop Proceeds	$10,000		Gift Shop Inventory	$2,500
Volunteer Time	$10,000		Run Gift Shop and Bingo	$0
Weekly Bingo Games	$15,000			
Total Resources	$67,500		Total Expenses	$67,500

The second table shows a balanced budget. It also shows several income streams and implies community support through the work of volunteers and the success of the bingo game fund-raising activity. A narrative discussion could be attached that would address the pending grant request from the local arts council. Is it regular contributor to the museum? When are funding announcements expected? What is known about the amount of competition for the funds? Why is this a reasonable amount to request?

Also note that the application made to the arts council will show the amount requested in this table as a pending grant application.

A Sources and Uses table also distinguishes between line items that might be matched in differing proportions by the grantor. In any case of a funder that requires a match for a project, the budget table would explicitly show the match even if other funding breakdowns are not required.

ITEM	FUNDING REQUEST	CASH MATCH	IN-KIND MATCH	TOTAL RESOURCES
Computer and software	$2,000 = 50%	$2,000 = 50%	0	$4,000
Staff time	$15,000 = 50%	$15,000	$5,000 = Volunteer time	$35,000
Audit costs	0	0	$25,000 = donated service by board member	$25,000
Training costs	$2,000	0	0	$2,000
Total costs	$19,000	$17,000	$30,000	$66,000

In this example, there is a mix of matching scenarios. This is not an uncommon situation, where certain types of expenses will require cash match and other expenses are allowed to have in-kind match, as well as by differing matching levels. Matching is often stipulated as a percentage, for example "25 percent cash match" or "10 percent match, including in-kind" or as a ratio such as "$1 match for each $3 grant funds" or "one-to-one match." Watch for rules about the amount of value that may be attributed to a volunteer's time when allowed as part of the matching contribution. Also be careful with the math if the cash match ratio is different from the allowable in-kind match when both are allowed.

For a good example of a budget narrative combined with a budget table, we recap the sample budget from the fictional J. M. McCoy Health Center application seen at the beginning of the chapter. It fully explains the line items and sources of funds and how these expenses relate to the program.

EXAMPLE OF BUDGET AND PROJECT SUSTAINABILITY NARRATIVE

The J. M. McCoy Health Center, Continued

6. Budget and Long-Term Sustainability

The capital improvements to the building are nearly complete, and the center should be able to open in six months. These are being given to the center as in-kind donations. The budget therefore reflects nearly all operational costs. Only a few pieces of equipment remain to be purchased and will be purchased through the separate capital campaign.

MCCOY HEALTH CENTER OPERATIONS BUDGET SUMMARY TABLE 1

Item	Cost per Unit	Extended Cost for Year
Salaries and Fringes	$60,000 ea	$120,000
Utilities/Telephone/Internet	$1,000/month	$12,000
Office Supplies	$500/month	$6,000
Medical Supplies, donated	$1,000/month	$0
Medical Supplies, purchased	$2,000/month	$24,000
Volunteer Recognition Program	$100 ea	$250
Insurance, property	$1,000	$1,000
Cleaning and Maintenance	$250/month	$3,000
Total Year		$166,250

Revenues to the center will be limited, as most of the expected patients will not have access to health insurance. Medical education classes charge a nominal $5 per class fee, and one partner organization, Mill Quarter Veterans of America, has pledged to provide ten scholarships each month to those who cannot afford this amount. Total income expected: $1,200 per year. Other pledges for this year include:

- The United Appeal has pledged: $50,000
- The Central Ohio Community Foundation has pledged: $45,000

EXAMPLE OF BUDGET AND PROJECT SUSTAINABILITY NARRATIVE

The Donor Relations Committee, a special committee of five volunteers and headed up by one of the board members, is responsible for special fund-raising to create an endowment to cover some of the long-term overhead and maintenance expenses of the center. Currently this includes direct appeals to community members and donation boxes that will be distributed to supportive businesses in the community, as well as in the center itself. Though patients will not be charged for services, they will have the opportunity to contribute something anonymously at the donation boxes. Other large fund-raisers will be planned, as well as solicitation of legacy gifts (contributions directly from the estates of deceased supporters) as the committee becomes more organized. The plan is to raise $500,000 per year for the next six years, and with cautious investment management, this should generate enough investment income to fund operations at current levels after that time.

The center does not expect to become totally financially independent. There will always be a need for some support from the community and special opportunity grants. The Donor Relations Committee, as well as the board of directors and the executive director, will have responsibility for maintaining relationships with community stakeholders and community connection to and awareness of the beneficial work of the center.

CHAPTER SUMMARY

- Obtain accurate estimates of all costs.
- Present the requested level of budget detail.
- Obtain source documentation of cost estimates.
- Properly attribute the value of volunteer time.
- Check the math; sources and uses should add up.
- Be sure that matching fund thresholds have been met.
- Write a narrative explaining budget items, if required.
- Budgets are especially suited for presentation in table format.

  - Label columns and rows clearly and accurately.
  - Be consistent in use of decimals, dollar signs, and spaces.
  - Watch for instructions about rounding.

- Do not make excessive requests; match request with typical awards and funder.

$2.25
$4.25
Smoothies
bananas
mangoes
blueberries
raspberries or
strawberries
$3.75

CHAPTER 12

ESTABLISH THE ORGANIZATION'S QUALIFICATIONS

CASE STUDY: DIANNE HARRIS

Hope for New Life's organizers claimed to be teachers in the local public school system. Because their plans were so incomplete in so many other ways, I never got around to asking for their teaching certificates or areas of expertise. They did not offer any information about previous nonprofit management experience, business or accounting skills, or experience with adult learners or the "welfare to work" regulations.

Furthermore, they did not seem to be pursuing partners with the expertise they might need to conduct their project. The only help they sought was someone who would be so eloquent and experienced in grant writing that the city would deliver the $9 million in funding. I was reluctant to spend the good favor I had accumulated with funders and the city council by trying to make a case for a project and organization that was at the time so unqualified for funding.

— Dianne Harris

In contrast, the microbusiness development project was being sponsored by a long-established community development agency, with several successful grant programs to its credit. The instructional staff members at the technical college were credentialed in their fields and had been teaching these classes for many years. The local business association was willing to be a partner in referring prospects to the program. The grant application included résumés of all key staff, copies of the curriculum, and listed the accrediting agencies of the college and the program.

Most grants require a section that describes the applicant organization and the experience and qualifications of those who will be involved with the program. This is another way the funder can judge the ability of the organization to effectively carry out the program and sustain itself in the future. Just as an employer looks for skills that relate to the job it is are filling, the funder is looking for skills related to the actual service to be provided, as well as management and financial skills. It is not unusual for members of the board of directors to provide some of the oversight and needed expertise, so their qualifications are important, too. This chapter shows how to easily present the organization and its qualifications.

TABLE OF ORGANIZATION

Not all funders will ask for a presentation of a table of organization, also sometimes called a table of authority. Even if they do not, it is an element that is effective as a graphical representation of the structure of the organization. If they do, it is not necessary to show every single position that will be active in a program. If some staff members have roles in more than one division of an organization, this can sometimes be shown under both divisions with a link. If this relationship is on purpose to facilitate coordination of different activities, it is possible to show them only once, with links drawn from this person to their contacts or roles in the different divisions. The human resources division of the organization may already have a table drawn up, in which case it can be easily copied and inserted into the grant request. If not already available, begin to think about roles and responsibilities of various staff members and how they interrelate. Outline the basic levels of decision-making responsibilities and who reports to whom. There may be new relationship pathways to be created for a new program, so be sure to fully think through the structural changes that may be needed to effectively accomplish the goals of the program.

The physical representation does not have to incorporate boxes or bubbles; the information may easily be displayed in a simple table created in a word processing program. To use boxes or bubbles, special software with some drawing capabilities is needed to produce an electronic version. Each step may show the title and name of the person, including a short programmatic title.

This is an example of an organization chart that can be created using the "Diagram" command found under the "Insert" menu in Microsoft Word:

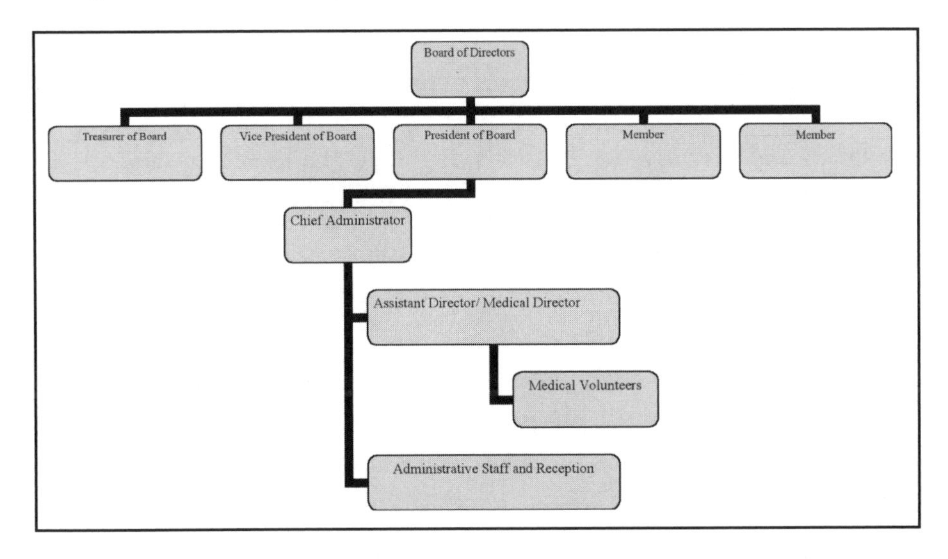

RÉSUMÉS

Most funders will want some description of the organization's key volunteers and staff's qualifications and experience to implement the program and to responsibly manage the grant funds. In the program description some reference will have been made showing the board, staff, and volunteer responsibilities in general and specifically pertaining to this program. In the qualifications section, the narrative goes on to demonstrate their education, training, and experience that specifically qualify them to perform the functions needed for the program. Here and in the budget, address the amount of work they currently are responsible for and how they will be able to take on the additional responsibilities. When staff or services cannot be hired till funding is acquired, it helps to demonstrate that the position will be quickly filled with qualified people. This can be done by including a position description that outlines experience and qualification requirements. A few organizations I have known have actually recruited candidates or contract employees but withheld actual hiring contingent on funding of their program. The main problem with this technique is that, depending on the time involved, it is difficult to ensure that these same candidates will still be available when funding is achieved. However, when it can be done, the program will be able to start up more quickly, since the recruiting and hiring process is already completed.

For board and executive-level officers, highlight the leadership and special skills they bring to this organization. Be sure to mention other boards and committees they may have served on, professional credentials, awards, certifications, and education they have earned, as well as past employment.

The grant guidelines may require a short narrative to show these qualifications and roles in the project, a submission of formal résumés, or both. Most professionals will have résumés that can be provided easily. If not available, it may be necessary to interview them for the purpose of creating their résumé for the application. Address vacant positions that are important to the program, how functions are currently being attended to, and the organization's efforts to locate and recruit a well-qualified person for the role.

CERTIFICATION

Some grant guidelines will ask for submitted copies of licenses or certificates as documentation that board or staff have the qualifications needed to practice certain professions, such as an MD (Medical Doctor) or RN (Registered Nurse). Request that these be provided to the grant writer and have the affected person sign a release statement indicating that he or she knows these materials will be presented to the funding organization. The releases, which show the person that his or her privacy will not be violated, will not necessarily be required in the grant proposal but should be kept in personnel or grant-related files.

Qualifications and experience apply to the organization itself, as well as the staff. Describe the amount of experience the organization has running this or similar programs in the past. How long has it operated? How has it succeeded in meeting its prior goals? How has the program evolved, grown, or improved? Has it won any awards or recognition? Has there been any positive media coverage of the organization or its projects? Incorporate this type of history into the narrative on qualifications.

EXAMPLE OF AN ORGANIZATION BACKGROUND SECTION

5. Organizational Capacity and Qualifications

The founding board of the J. M. McCoy Health Center formed more than a year ago due to concerns about the healthcare needs of the Mill Quarter neighborhood. The center holds a tax-exempt status under Section 501(c)(3) of the IRS code. The board of directors now consists of five highly qualified individuals who donate their time to establishing and running the center. Two part-time registered nurses, who also have administrative experience, serve as the center's chief administrator and assistant manager, with at least one providing coverage during all hours of operation. Volunteer medical board certified nurse practitioners and physicians provide the actual medical evaluations and treatments and prescribe any necessary medications. The full résumés of key individuals are available on request. These key individuals and their roles are as follows:

Board President	Harriet Smith, MD, Women's Health Center
Board Vice-President	Harold Smose, MD, All Saint's Hospital Psychiatry Department
Board Treasurer	Harry Jones, CPA, Smith & Jones LLC
Board Member	Hazel Thoms, Ph.D., Professor of Foreign Languages, All Saint's College
Board Member	Henrietta Toopes, Owner, Best Ever Cookie Company
Chief Administrator	Hubert Underwood, RN, MBA
Assistant Director	Hallie Ulrich, RN

CHAPTER SUMMARY

The qualifications sections for a grant program will include some or all of the following:

- Organizational chart
- Résumés
- Licenses or certificates
- Plans to fill vacancies
- Position descriptions
- Narrative description of the role of each person involved and relationships to others

CHAPTER 13

SUSTAINABILITY: HOW WILL THE PROGRAM CONTINUE WHEN THE GRANT IS OVER?

CASE STUDY: DIANNE HARRIS

I see some difference in local government styles when I help them with community development grants. Sometimes one prefers to work only through a contract with a consultant to write and administer the programs. These are usually for a single project or a defined set of limited projects. Because it does not envision an ongoing community development program, it prefers to engage someone for a limited period of time that already has significant experience and success with the programs.

When the program is over, the contract is complete and we part ways, at least for a while. Other communities are comfortable with making community development an integral part of their function and use some of the consulting time for assistance in setting up a department, hiring and training staff, and setting an agenda for the future. In this case they must be assured of sustained funding for these positions and other overhead costs into the future. Part of this strategy may be to continue to pursue a number of government grants, generation of program income, and perhaps anticipated additional revenues that may flow from increased economic activity in the community that this department will stimulate. For example, this department may be instrumental in revitalizing a vacant building so that it now generates more tax revenue, attracting a new industry to the community that will increase income tax revenue, or instituting a new set of fees or hotel bed taxes for the purpose of funding a tourism department. By planning for sustainability,

CASE STUDY: DIANNE HARRIS

they use their grant funds as investments to leverage the continued improvement of the community, in contrast to the simple accomplishment of a single objective.

— Dianne Harris

Is there a plan for continuing the proposed program when this grant is over? What funding can be expected in the future? Believe it or not, although some funders provide for re-funding successful programs in the future, most grantors will not want to adopt a program in perpetuity. They view themselves as catalysts to helping their applicants get started with a new endeavor that will become self-sustaining through other means so that they can amplify the impact of their funds. In the grant guidelines it should state whether or not previously funded organizations will be considered for additional awards. Sometimes it will re-fund for a limited number of times or, conversely, award additional funds only after some defined waiting period. Guidelines will indicate their reasons for this policy. Sometimes a previous grant recipient may be eligible for additional funds only when starting a new activity that also meets the funding criteria.

Some grant guidelines will ask for a separate section describing how the program will be sustained in the future, when the grant funds are exhausted. Otherwise, this should be briefly outlined in the general program description section. It is important to provide information on sustainability strategies even if not specifically asked for.

In the case of a demonstration program, there may not be an intention to run the program for more than one grant cycle. In that situation address future roles and the purpose of the organization, how information gathered from the demonstration program will be communicated to other organizations, how sharing the successes and experiences of this program will occur, and what assistance may be available to or needed by others in setting up and running a similar effort.

In this section the writer will recap other fund-raising efforts and plans, along with a list of timed gifts and major donor commitments for the future, if any. In Chapter 2 several methods, in addition to grant applications, were outlined that might be employed to raise funds. When a funder asks to be shown that the program is sustainable, put grant-seeking tactics in the context of a larger strategy that includes other sources of funds to support this activity into the future. Relationships that indicate that re-funding can be expected can be divulged.

If you are working on building an endowment for the program, discuss the progress and long-term and intermediate goals for the endowment fund. Explain the actual fund-raising effort, including how donors will be contacted, the volunteer, staff, or board involvement, and any investment plans for managing the endowment. The grant instructions may ask for identification of major donor commitments that have already been secured. If it is anticipated that some amount of income may be generated from the program, such as participant fees, these may be used to leverage commitments for future funds. If more grants will need to be secured from other sources in the future, mention the foundations or agencies that management's research and established relationships indicate may possibly give future funding.

If this is indeed a one-time program, it may be necessary to present what will happen to various resources acquired for the program. Will they be disposed of through auction or donation to others? If sold in some way, how will the proceeds be used? The funder may require that any program income generated, including the sale of equipment and furnishings, be returned to the foundation funds. Government grants, in particular, have firm rules about how capital equipment and real estate are to be disposed of and what records must be maintained.

CHAPTER SUMMARY

- Plan for the future of the program.
- Identify future sources to approach for grants.
- Identify potential revenues from the program.
- Explain the plan for future fund-raising.
- Identify pledges of major gifts.
- If a demonstration program, explain planned communications and technical assistance needed to replicate the program elsewhere.
- If the program will end, show how capital equipment will be used or sold and what will happen to the income generated.

CHAPTER 14

ENHANCEMENTS & SUPPORTING DOCUMENTATION

A great deal of supporting documentation may be included with the application package, though it may be too lengthy to incorporate into the main narrative. This material may be packaged at the end in the appendices. This chapter reviews the submission of video or photographic material and other required documentation.

Material that might appear in an appendix if not requested specifically in other sections include: copies of lengthy résumés of staff and board members, newspaper articles, brochures, letters of support, plans and drawings of construction projects, the IRS 501(c)(3) determination of nonprofit status letter, resolutions, annual budget, annual reports, annual audits, signed letters of pledged in-kind services or materials, other proof of matching funds, and/or any other material that strengthens or reinforces the claims made in the narrative.

Government and large foundations may supply a list of materials that they require to be included in the appendices.

Unless there are specific and tight restrictions on the length or size of the package, some additional materials can be helpful, even if not requested in the guidelines. This material might include copies of outreach and promotional materials that you use; publicity such as newspaper articles that help your funder to see that you have community recognition; copies of résumés and certificates for special training or education, which are strong indicators of the abilities of your staff and board members; thank you letters from your past clients, which can put a human face on the benefits to the community that you claim; letters of support from other community leaders and organizations, which are sometimes still helpful and sometimes specifically discouraged. Politicians can have a tendency to write these for anybody, diluting their effectiveness, or maybe not write support letters for anyone, which unfairly penalizes good programs where support letters may be a competitive element. Unless forbidden, it can still be effective to include a few well-written support letters from members of the community who are familiar with the good things your group accomplishes.

Accumulating these materials takes a little effort and again can be a part of your ongoing work so that you have a reserve of material to use whenever needed. A staff member or volunteer could be given the responsibility of being the group's historian. In that role, he or she may routinely take photos and videos of group events and willing participants. The historian may collect into a sort of scrapbook any media pieces, letters, and cards that address the quality of your work. Even letters of support generated for previous applications and glowing performance reviews by any accrediting agency can be a part of the scrapbook and available material that helps to establish your credibility as a quality provider that deserves more funding.

New letters of support can be a bit of a nuisance to gather, especially if they are required. You may be working under a deadline, and your priorities are not necessarily those of the person you have contacted for support. You may have inadvertently made the contact just a day after the person has left for a well deserved three-week vacation in a far-off place, or be off on an extended medical leave. You can achieve better results if this is someone with whom you already have an established relationship and he or she understands and supports your work. Without that prior relationship, the person you have asked for support may feel they should, as a matter of integrity, research you and your organization before crafting a letter. Even with a prior relationship, you can help them to help you by providing a "sample" letter that addresses all the key issues that your letters need to emphasize. Agreeable people will simply fax a well-done letter that you provide onto their letterhead and then sign it. This particular issue is another area where it is directly helpful to have built up a network of contacts, and you should not ignore making sure elected officials are aware of you and your work. The problem of time means that contacts to request letters of support should occur as soon as you know you will need them. If a promised source falls through, do you have acceptable backup letters available? If "clean" originally signed letters are needed in your application, then that means you must also provide enough time for delivery of the letter before you package the application. If couriers or overnight delivery services are used, it increases the cost of completing the application, though this can still be regarded as worthwhile for a prospective large grant award. Sometimes, though not as professional, you may rely on a faxed signed letter but still have the original delivered to you to retain in the event of a question or for use in another application at a later time.

The following is a sample of an application of the type that requires supplemental materials.

SAMPLE INDIVIDUAL GRANT

APPLICATION FOR FACADE IMPROVEMENT GRANT PROGRAM

1. Applicant Name:__Joe Joe Smith__________________Phone:_555-5555____
2. Applicant Federal ID # (or SSN):__xx-xxxxxxx____________________________
3. Business Name:__Joe Joe's Java House____________________________
4. Building Location Address:__100 West Ave. ___________________________
5. Contact Mailing Address:__P.O. Box xxxx, Anytown, Anystate_00000__

SAMPLE INDIVIDUAL GRANT

6. Estimated Project Cost:__$10,000______________________________

7. Amount of Grant Requested (limited to 50% of cost up to $5,000)__$5,000___

8. Source of Matching Funds: Cash, Borrowing

9. Description of the condition of the building and the work proposed to be done with the grant and matching funds. Attach photos and schematic drawings drawn to scale: The awnings of the café have become torn, faded, and dirty. The paint around the windows, shutters, doors, and trim is flaking. The old sign was damaged in the last hailstorm and no longer reflects the character of the business. Some of the mortar is missing from between the bricks, and the masonry needs re-tuckpointed in some areas. The proposed work includes: replacement of the canvas part of the awning with the same profile, changing the color to dark brown, with four-inch tall lettering in beige. Lettering to include the name "Joe Joe's Java House," 100 West Avenue. The door, trim, and shutters will be scraped and repainted in a taupe color, number 333 on the paint sample chart provided. A bricklayer will mix mortar to match the color and composition of the original and apply using standard tuckpointing procedures on the affected façade area (roughly 10 percent of the total façade area.)

10. I hereby certify that the grant funds requested will be used only for the work described on this application; furthermore I certify that the work will address or abate a substandard condition of the building and will be consistent with the requirements of the Downtown Historic District Design Standards.

Signature:__Joe Joe Java______________ Date:___xx-xx-xxxx__________

For Office Use Only:

Date Submitted for Local Design Standard Review:________________

Approved Date:_________________

Date Submitted to State Historic Preservation Officer for Review:__________

Approved Date:_________________ (attach copy of letter)

Zoning Clearance Obtained:_______________By:_________________

Grant Approved:__________________Date:____________________

The above is an example of the type of application that might be used for local grant funding for a business fix-up program. These types of programs are among the few that sometimes provide actual grant assistance to a business. This application format is purposely simple to reduce barriers to program participation, which is desirable to achieve the goal of improving the look of Anytown's downtown.

It does require attachments of photos of the current conditions and drawings illustrating the work to be done. The applicant has done a good job by providing color choice information, because the community has design regulations in the historic area. The color choices would have to be approved as a condition of receiving the grant funds. By providing this information up front, the applicant increases his chance of being funded by demonstrating that he will comply with regulations affecting the property and the grant. He has also carefully complied with the budget limits for the request and met the matching funds requirement.

Some towns make this type of application form and detailed information about the fix-up program available on a Web site. More frequently the program manager will want the applicant to call or drop in to discuss the proposal and requirements prior to submission. Sometimes these types of local funds may have open-ended application periods but are limited in amount. As with any grant, it is helpful to obtain information about availability prior to going through the work of preparing even a simple submission.

If the funder specifically requests that videos and photos not be included, abide by those wishes. Some prefer to have only one-part applications or to not give a less technologically gifted group an unfair disadvantage. However, it is common for arts-related awards to encourage or even require photographic material documenting previous work produced by the artist(s) as evidence of style and skill. Other useful visuals might include concept sketches of the proposed artwork or construction projects. Videos can provide a high-impact statement about your work, incorporating color, design, spoken statements, graphics, music, or recordings of performances. Visuals can highlight the special details of a historic structure and its historic function in the community that is part of the project. They can record clients and staff while actively engaged in their roles or making statements about special features of your work that they have found especially beneficial or rewarding, perhaps even commenting on the professionalism and caring nature of the staff. A performance group might include segments from a recent performance or practice sessions and also include interviews with performers, coaches, or critics. An author might obtain a recording of a reading of some of his or her recent work, or a workshop that he or she contributed to. Visual images powerfully convey a wealth of information and impressions about your work and allow the reviewer a quick insight into your operation that might be available otherwise only through a lengthy site visit.

TIPS: *It is helpful to use a medium that is compatible with commonly available viewing equipment. The more professionally the video presentation can be planned and executed, the more effective it will be. Hiring a professional production crew can be cost prohibitive. Therefore, be sure to find out if any members of staff, volunteers, or even board members have any skills in this area. College students in communications and media programs can also be a resource for production as a special student project. When packaging the application, it can help to create a unified visual presentation, through color, logos, and use of fonts, and use these elements on labels (also indicating that each piece is one of X number total in the complete application package), title pages, and other parts of the submission. They will assist the reviewers in keeping unattached parts of a submission together.*

Also remember to obtain and file signed waivers or permission statements from anyone who appears in a video or photograph that you wish to use.

If the subject is a minor child, a parent or guardian should provide this waiver for you.

EXAMPLE OF WAIVER TO USE PHOTOGRAPHIC IMAGES

Hypothetical Jones Dance Company

(on your letterhead)

Date:____________________

I, __________________________________ (name of subject or parent of minor child) hereby acknowledge that the Jones Dance Company as well as members of the press may photograph or record part or all of various practice sessions or performances. These may be for the purpose of creation of a portfolio, or for use in publicity materials, news releases, or materials developed for the purposes of obtaining donor or foundation support.

I hereby provide my permission for myself or my child (_______________________) to be included in these recordings and photos and release the Jones Dance Company from any further obligation to notify me that any such photograph or recordings have been or are planned to be made and/or used in the manners listed above.

I understand that the Jones Dance Company does not plan to nor does this release give it the rights to use my or my child's image in any production that is made for sale and distribution to the general public and/or for the purpose of generating revenue for the Jones Dance Company from the sales of this material.

Signed:____

Printed Name:____

Name of Minor Child if Applicable:_____________________________

Date Signed:____

Notarized By:____

CHAPTER SUMMARY

- Assemble lengthy material into an appendix or accessory submission packet.
- Marketing materials, financial reports, and support letters and partnership commitments are commonly included.
- Arts projects may require photographic evidence of prior work, as well as concepts of the proposal.
- Material that cannot be physically attached to the primary narrative should have a common design element and be well labeled.

CHAPTER 15

FINAL SUBMISSION & WAITING

THE FUNDER'S PERSPECTIVE, CONTINUED

CASE STUDY: AN

"The objectives of each funder will be different, and the emphasis on technical aspects of the submission will vary a great deal. We have funded groups whose functions are somewhat unusual and do not fit neatly into one of our categories.

"Because of that, their responses to our online application questions may appear somewhat weak, but if they serve an important role in the community, they will still score well with us. We understand that, in our community, small arts groups are all volunteers, may not have grant writing expertise, may not have access to computers, and cannot afford to buy this expertise. Our executive director has been known to provide guidance on how to fill out the application form, although she does not write the application for them. Of course, other foundations might not have the same perspective or may have too many applicants to provide such assistance."

— AN

This chapter presents recommendations for producing an effective final appearance and the production and submission of the grant application, as well as some tips for staying sane while awaiting the funding announcements. After all the narratives have been written and supporting documents gathered, the applicant must still attend to several important steps. Do not let a messy presentation or missing sections detract from the quality of the grant proposal. AN's community-based foundation is forgiving of small community arts organizations that may lack grant proposal skills. It regards the consultations it gives as part of the technical assistance it provides to promote the arts. National foundations that receive many proposals may not provide much assistance.

The simplest of instructions may be the hardest to follow: Check and recheck the document and the application guidelines and instructions. Carefully and meticulously follow all directions given by the funder for submission. If a limit is imposed on length, edit out unnecessary material. If a particular format is stipulated, such as single- or double-spacing between lines or font sizes, be sure to comply. Some grant makers will request more than one copy, and be sure to keep at least one for your own records as well. Though this book has demonstrated the usual method of organization for the table of contents, transmittal (cover) letter, abstract, narratives, and appendices, if the funder has instructed the use of a different organization, use its preferred sequence. For short applications, the use of expensive binding is not necessary. A simple binder clip or three-hole-punched folder or binder will securely hold the documents but allow the review team to easily make additional copies or divvy up the material for review. However, this is another point that can vary and should be watched for in the submission instructions.

If the organization has access to publication software and has members skilled in desktop publication, by all means use them. However, the most important design advice is simply to be neat in appearance. Avoid the temptation to mix more than two or three fonts, and use them consistently throughout the document, such as one for titles, one for subtitles, and the last for the main text. Using too many fonts tends to look amateurish and detract from the sense of accomplishment that is the desired effect. Allow for generous margins and spacing between sections. White space has a pleasing effect and makes documents easier to read. If computers or word processors are not available, try to avoid cross-outs and globs of correction fluid.

Some organizations are beginning to accept or even require electronic application submissions. For example, the Dayton Foundation, a community foundation serving Dayton, Ohio and its immediate surroundings, uses an electronic submission for letters of inquiry. After completing the Web-based form and pressing the "submit" button, there is an immediate return message as to whether the project is eligible and further instructions on how to proceed. In these situations the applicant loses the opportunity to enhance or distinguish its impact with a distinctive image. Also, once the "submit" button is activated, it may not be possible to recall the application if an error is discovered. So, whether preparing a written proposal or a Web-based proposal, the need for careful editing to correct content or typographical mistakes before that final step is equally important.

In Chapter 5 steps were outlined for getting organized at the start of the grant process. Try to eliminate the potential for catastrophe, or at least have contingency plans. What will happen if the copier breaks down? What if a courier is unable to enter a government building that has extremely high security? The application package must get to the funder on time. Failure to arrive on time could mean the application will not even be accepted for consideration, especially when working with government agencies. Last, make a copy of the application for your own files.

To review from Chapter 5's recommendations for an outline, the common organization of the grant sections are as follows:

1. Cover Letter

2. Project Abstract

3. Needs Statement

4. Program Description

5. Goals, Objectives, and Evaluation Plan

6. Organizational Qualifications

7. Budget

8. Program Sustainability

9. Appendices

After the grant application, next is the most agonizing part of the process, waiting for notification that you have won your grant award.

WERE WE FUNDED?

The National Endowment for the Arts Web site, **www.NEA.gov**, has a nice graphic showing the "grant life cycle;" beginning with publication of the guidelines, submission of the application, and in its case a three-tier review — first by staff, second by a panel, and last by the National Council and Chairman — and finally notification of the applicants of their awards. It is useful to help visualize what is happening to your application after you have submitted it.

If not stated in the guidelines, try to get information from the funder as to the time for review and making its funding decisions and announcements. The review period can take as little as a week or as long as six months. This possible lag in availability of crucial funding could have an impact on the program budget or timing of implementation. Your financial and budget planning should have this waiting period built in. Do not expect to be reimbursed by the pending grant for funds spent prior to obtaining the grant agreement. Most funders do not allow for it.

In the interim, use the time to finish up other projects, become organized, and be ready to begin immediately on funding award. Devote time to taking care of the rest of the organization's business, attending conferences, scheduling doctor's appointments, or perhaps attending to tasks that were ignored during the grant writing process. Do not harass the reviewing agency with frequent calls about the status of the proposal. However, if a week has passed since the expected award date, it is acceptable to contact it with a single polite inquiry about when it expects to announce awards. E-mail, if available, is a good way to make this contact without imposing on the funder's staff time.

Some reviews, especially for federal grants, are conducted by review teams that are not familiar with any of the applicants or the areas they serve. This can be purposeful to avoid inadvertently slanting a review score based on personal preferences or friendships. Sometimes a reviewer will not be fully versed in the discipline that your work involves, and the names of various organizations and projects may be similar. Therefore, when communicating with a reviewer with questions about the status or scoring of your application, completely identify yourself so that he or she is able to locate your information without confusion with another. If, after the review is complete, there is the opportunity to obtain the scoring of the application received or additional commentary on the ranking of the application, do so and learn from the experience for the next submission to this or other funders. This should be done whether the application was successful or not.

Grant award announcements may be made by mail, telephone, news release, or gossip. Government grant awards are announced only after the communities' legislators have been informed. The legislators are given the honor of making the announcement to the media — and sometimes they even think to tell their grant winner! Normally, the winners will be informed first. However, once I learned about a successful application for one of my programs only by reading about it in the local newspaper after the congressman made the press release. He had not called the community because he thought the reviewing agency was going to contact us.

If not already done by the legislator or funding agency, be sure to make announcements to the media, on your Web site, in your newsletters, and to your donors, the board of directors, any partners involved in the project, and especially your staff when you learn you have received a grant. They will like to share in your celebration. It will also begin the outreach to the public, letting them know that your new project is about to begin or continue for another year. The publicity will help to raise the public perception of your group or your work and will contribute to your ability to secure additional donations and funding in the future. Also be sure to save articles and award letters for your scrapbook.

If the news was not good, use it as a learning experience. As soon as possible schedule a review conference to see how the application might be strengthened in the future. Are there comments that will help with applications that may be underway to other funders? Sometimes in spite of producing a strong and professional application, you are just at the mercy of the degree of need experienced by others in a highly competitive grant cycle. I believe that some funds I have applied for in the past had a "secret" number of points awarded for how many times you had already submitted. If a group were to give up on funds where it had scored well in spite of not receiving the funds, it might lose those "tenacity" points. Strategize with your team on how to best proceed while new sources of funds are being explored. Do not get discouraged or become resentful.

CASE STUDY: JM

"I was frustrated once upon having to resubmit an application to the same program three times over an 18-month period before attaining funding. Since then every application that has been submitted for them has been funded. Tell people that persistence works and that they should not give up."

—JM

CHAPTER SUMMARY

- Follow directions.
- Check for mistakes.
- Be neat.
- Limit the number of fonts used.
- Use white space for a pleasing appearance.
- Have contingency plans.
- Deliver on time.
- Patiently wait.
- Find out the expected time to review proposals and make decisions.
- Build this time into the program work plan.
- Do not expect to be reimbursed for expenditures made prior to the grant award.
- Use the waiting time productively.
- Study the scoring criteria in advance of preparing grant if possible.

Winning the Grant Is Not The End

CHAPTER 16

YOU WANT TO KNOW WHAT? POST-GRANT REQUIREMENTS

This case study focuses on the issue of post-grant performance. The experience of "Town M" and the experience of " City G" demonstrate the necessity of showing good performance after the grant award.

CASE STUDY: TOWN M

I once wrote a grant for a town we will call Town M, so as not to embarrass it. The grant was for Federal Transportation Enhancement funds that were being distributed through the region's Municipal Planning Organization (MPO). MPOs, by the way, are transportation planning districts designated for federal and state transportation planning purposes.

Its needs were simple, to install sidewalks along a busy state route that went through the center of town and led to the town swimming pool and county fairgrounds at the edge of town. Several small businesses and convenience stores were located along this stretch of road. Residents, including children, walked in the grass to these various destinations and had worn an actual path. The rough path made access to wheelchair users virtually impossible. In the winter when snow was on the ground, the pedestrians would move to the roadway itself.

An eligible use of the grant funds was to promote pedestrian and other non-vehicle transportation, enhance safety, and eliminate barriers for disabled travelers. It required a local match, and the town engineer would provide all the design work needed at no cost to the grant funds.

CASE STUDY: TOWN M

Most transportation-related grants are straightforward in requiring mostly a presentation of data, with only simple narratives, to demonstrate the need for the project. Certified cost estimates and a few photos or documentation such as proof of control of the site, are part of the submitted application package.

The staff members and I pulled all the information together, created an organized and easy-to-read package, and submitted a request for approximately $80,000, which was approved. My work was through, and this being a construction project, the responsibility for implementing the grant fell to the town's engineer and public safety director.

Imagine my surprise when I visited almost a year later and there was no indication that the project had started. I called the mayor's office to ask about its status. The engineer and public safety director failed to pay attention to required progress time schedules. The design drawings were not submitted by the deadline, and the grant was revoked and the funds given to another community. Having failed to perform the first step in the process seriously hurt Town M's opportunity to resubmit for the funds again. It made the town appear either incapable of implementing the project, not truly in need of the project, or both. I'm not sure those sidewalks were ever built. Not only did it lose the free money, it wasted its time and cost of making the application, and the citizens likely still stumble along that muddy path to their destinations.

The Lesson: Town M's experience shows that the post-grant period is very important. When making an application, be sure the project can be completed within the required time period and that required progress milestones are met.

CASE STUDY: CITY G

City G, a small rural city, applied for a large grant to correct housing code violations for its elderly and low income residents. This would have the effect of making the homes safer and more energy efficient for the residents and also to make significant visual improvements in neighborhoods that were beginning to appear run-down and were losing property value.

The city leaders obtained these funds, which were also federal in origin, from their state department of development and made them available to low income and elderly residents as grants that would be repayable only if the property was sold in fewer than five years. In this way they hoped to preserve the improvements to the benefit of the low income residents, rather than create an unreasonable level of profit

CASE STUDY: CITY G

for potential investors. (This is also an example of how a grant program design can be structured to serve the need identified and avoid spending valuable funds on unintended beneficiaries.)

The staff responsible for implementing the program worked hard at outreach to the community and was able to quickly acquire enough eligible applicants. Sound construction management allowed the projects to be completed in a timely manner, and budgets were adhered to well. The state Department of Development (DOD) staff evaluated the program, toured some of the homes worked on, and were satisfied that the program had accomplished all stated goals and managed the funds properly.

However, near the end, the staff had one unhappy decision to make. There remained two applicants that were in great need and only enough remaining funds to serve one. The established criteria for prioritizing projects clearly indicated which family would be assisted, but staff felt badly that the sole remaining applicant would not be able to receive the help. This was a one-time program that would not be available again for a long time, if ever. Imagine their surprise and delight when the state DOD staff called up to say that they had "recovered" some funds unexpectedly that needed to be spent right away, and could City G use another $20,000, since it had done such a good job? The answer was a resounding "yes," and the final applicant was assisted.

Analysis: "Recovered" funds is the polite way of saying that a grantee did not perform well and lost its grant funds, much like happened to Town M in the first example. Although the grantee cannot count on miracles to happen as did for City G, it is common that good performance will be rewarded in some way — perhaps through bonus funds, an invitation to reapply in future grant rounds, or perhaps with some good publicity that will create more funding support from others at another time.

Once a grant has been awarded, the funder becomes a partner to the endeavor. Funders do not hand over a check and then disappear from the scene. Sometimes the funds are disbursed on a reimbursement basis only or in payments related to documented impending costs. That is one way the funder can ensure ongoing communication and the ability to monitor progress.

The money is free in that it does not have to be paid back — as long as the funds are used as intended. The funder has invested its money and often that of other donor organizations as well. It needs to be assured that its benevolent mission has indeed been accomplished by its support of a worthy program. This is not, however, an adversarial situation. Funders want their grantees to be successful and will provide a great deal of non-monetary support and advice during the grant period. The post-award period is another great time to strengthen communications between the funder and the grantee. It is a time to continue to strengthen the relationship in anticipation of further support in years to come.

THE GRANT AGREEMENT

One way the funder solidifies the relationship is by issuing a Memorandum of Understanding (MOU) or a Grant Agreement. The grant agreement is a working legal contract that both the funder and the applicant sign. Read and understand the fine print. Additional certification forms related to compliance with local, state, and federal regulations may need to be signed and returned. Contact the funder immediately if terms are not perfectly understood. Conditions on use of the funds, as well as program completion deadlines and status-reporting requirements, are covered in the agreement. A government grant agreement will be a very long and complex document and will formalize the amounts of the award, the source of the funds, the applicable governmental legislation and regulations governing the use of the funds, the completion date for use of the funds, and especially important, the numeric goals you said you would achieve. Smaller foundations may simply send an award letter congratulating you on your success and provide instructions for making draws against the grant funds. One client of mine said someone had opened the mail one day and a substantial check fell out for a grant application the organization had made many months ago and had forgotten it had even applied for. That was quite a surprise. I would advise, however, that you maintain a tracking system for the status of your grant applications, especially if you generate a lot of them. That is an element of good financial and operations management.

SITE VISITS

Another post-grant activity involves site visits from the funder. Sometimes these occur during grant evaluation. Sometimes site visits occur on grant award and sometimes later, after the program is operational. Sometimes a funder will make several visits throughout the program. The funder will want to see the facility where the services are being delivered. Try to keep it clean and tidy, even if clientele or the public are not received there. It must be kept according to any applicable health or fire codes. If inspections and permits are required on opening, be sure to schedule them and keep records and certificates of the reports where easily found. Some are even required to be kept posted in a conspicuous place, such as fire occupancy limits or elevator inspections. Framing of these certificates is not just a decorative touch; it helps to protect valuable documents from moisture in the air and other damage.

Staff and volunteers should be tidy and dressed according to their roles. Dress codes need only be in effect if necessary for health and safety, closed-toe shoes, for example. Office behaviors must be kept professional and respectful of the clients and each other. It is beneficial to have a relaxed and friendly environment for meeting the public as long as professionalism, respect, and confidentiality are maintained.

When site visits are anticipated, be sure to assemble any documents or staff the funder has indicated should be made available. For the purposes of site visits, as well as written status reports, establish a sound record-keeping system that is always kept up to date. This must be a priority. It does not take long to forget important details if they are not recorded immediately. Sign-in sheets are easy ways to keep tabs on the number of clients that use the service. Simple computer-based scheduling software or databases can track clients and demographic information. Client records can be simple written files, and a responsible person can be in charge of regular review and tallying of needed data. Set up a method to keep detailed records sufficient to track the measurable outcomes listed in the grant application, and use the evaluation plan from the proposal to measure the program's success, effectiveness, and indirect impact.

STATUS REPORTS

Status reports, if required, may be as simple as a letter that is submitted according to schedule or may be submitted on pre-printed forms. A status report will cover the following information:

- Identification of your organization: This may include a grant tracking number in addition to your name and address.
- The time period that the report is to cover
- The amount of funds that were awarded
- The amount of funds that have been drawn
- The balance available
- The stated numerical goals of the project
- The number of service units that have been delivered to date
- The number of services or cases that are in process at this time
- The number of cases on your waiting list
- Demographic information about those you have served to date
- A narrative description of efforts to keep the project on schedule and meet stated goals
- A signature line for the CEO of your organization to ensure that top management is aware of progress on the grant as well

The funder may have a reporting schedule that it is responsible for; for example, it may have to report to its board of directors or to donors at annual meetings. It will appreciate the grantee that understands the importance of submitting status reports on time and thoroughly completed. It helps to maintain a relationship with the funder; doing so will help strengthen the grantee's reputation for quality work. Failure to provide reports, especially after extended periods, or failure to use funds as described in the grant proposal could bring about bad news; this "free" money might have to be repaid (recaptured) if it is not spent according to "rules" for eligible expenses. This is especially true of grants that involve government funds.

SAMPLE STATUS REPORT			
Name of Grantee:	Grant Town, USA	Status Report #2	6 Months (of 12-month grant)
Address:	100 Main St.		
Contact Phone:	999-888-7777		
Project Budget:	$45,000	**Funds Expended to Date:**	$24,000
Units of Service Budgeted:	200 participants trained	**Units of Service Completed:**	100 participants trained
		Units in Progress:	25 registered for next conference
		Milestones Achieved:	Held one conference
Actions undertaken to complete objectives:	1. Repeat e-mail notice of conference	2. Obtained continuing education certification	3. Publicized in last newsletter

This is a sample of an interim report. The program period is half elapsed, and half of the goals have been met. The applicant states three actions toward completing the goals and can show that 25 of the needed 100 participants have registered for the second training conference. This could be interpreted as satisfactory progress on this project.

OTHER OBLIGATIONS

Some grants, especially residencies, may include a responsibility to share your expertise with your peer group through a conference presentation, an article for a newsletter, or maybe even an appearance in promotional materials for your benefactor. Grantors may ask you to provide a service to other disadvantaged groups that the funder has additional priorities to serve. This is a method for you to give back to your community and for your funder to leverage even greater benefits to a community for its cash investments. At any rate, any such responsibilities will be divulged before you apply so that you may decide if you are comfortable with this trade-off. It most certainly will be outlined in your grant award materials along with instructions as to when and how this obligation is to be fulfilled. If a conference appearance is required, the grantor must give you enough notice to make arrangements for your absence from your regular duties.

One example of a community that provides business grants is Abilene, Texas. The City of Abilene is a progressive city that passed a sales tax to provide, among other programs, several different purpose grants that serve large and small businesses alike. Each applicant is requested to contact the office prior to submission of an application. This preliminary contact must have the following information ready:

1. The number of new jobs to be created and the payscale of each job
2. The time expected to move from first hire to attainment of the goal employment
3. Position classification for each job created
4. Type of business

These instructions make it very clear that the purpose of Abilene's program is to increase employment in the area. Therefore the grant funds available will vary according to the number of jobs to be created or retained if the business does not close or relocate. This is another example of how a funder will design grant programs to meet priorities that it has dedicated itself to.

An example of how to report job creation information is as follows:

SAMPLE JOB CREATION REPORT			
Job Title	Number New Positions	Number Retained Positions	Pay Scale
Data Entry Clerk	2	2	$20,000-$30,000
Order Selectors	3	3	$12,000-$18,000

CHAPTER SUMMARY

- The funder's needs are also the grantee's needs.
- Use the grant agreement as a tool to manage the grant.
- Execute agreements, certifications, and other post-grant documents quickly.
- Operate the program and facilities well at all times.
- Preparation for site visits should not be difficult if record-keeping is attended to regularly.
- Obtain local permits and licenses, and keep them available and safe.
- Periodically extract statistics from the records and produce data for status reports.
- Track indirect benefits as well as stated measurable goals.
- Keep records of the grant funds themselves.

- Use this data, site visits, and status reports as opportunities to strengthen the organization's reputation and relationship with the funder for future grant requests.

APPENDIX

USEFUL WEB SITES FOR FINDING GRANTS

Alaska Individual Fellowships, The Rasmuson Foundation

www.rasmuson.org

American Masterpieces Grant Program, Vermont

http://vermontartscouncil.org/ArtsCalendarHome/tabid/273/Default.aspx#AM

Appalachian Festival of Plays

www.bartertheatre.com/festival

Center for Faith-Based and Community Initiatives

www.hhs.gov/fbci/

Charity Navigator

www.charitynavigator.org

The Chronicle of Philanthropy

www.philanthropy.com

Department of Commerce Grant Opportunities

www.commerce.gov/grants.html

Economic Research Institute

www.eri-nonprofit-salaries.com

Fund for Creative Communities

www.lmcc.net/grants/boroughwide/fundcreativecomm/index.html

Fellowship in Investigative Journalism

www.soc.american.edu

Finland Residency — Kemijarvi Art Residence

www.kemijarvi-artresidence.fi/indexeng.htm

Fundsnet Online Services

www.fundsnetservices.com

Firstgov

www.usa.gov

Foundation Center

www.foundationcenter.org

Writers in the Schools — Oregon Literary Arts

www.literary-arts.org/wits

Grantsmanship Center

www.tgci.com

GrantSmart

www.grantsmart.org

GoundWork Group

http://groundworkgroup.com

GuideStar

www.guidestar.org

Greater Pittsburgh Artist Opportunity Grants

http://pittsburghartscouncil.org/artistoppgrant.htm

Honoring Our Ancestors Grants

www.honoringourancestors.com/grants.html

Native Youth and Culture Fund

www.firstnations.org

The Authors League Fund

www.authorsleaguefund.org

Nickelodeon Writing Fellowship

www.nickwriting.com

Probonolink

http://probonolink.org

Ohio Grants

www.auditor.state.oh.us/LocalGovernmentServices/GrantResources/Default.htm

School Grants

www.schoolgrants.org

CONTESTS

Foreign Affairs: Travel Stories with a Twist

www.bcwriters.com/literary.php

Great American Think-Off

www.think-off.org

Write a Story for Children Competition

www.childrens-writers.co.uk/competition

COMPLETE GRANT PROPOSAL (RECAP OF THE HYPOTHETICAL J. M. MCCOY HEALTH CENTER)

Note: *This is a fictitious proposal. Neither the organization nor the staff members exist. Any similarity to actual persons or organizations is coincidental. However, the format is intended to demonstrate an effective method of submitting a proposal to a foundation for a human services activity.*

SAMPLE LETTER OF INQUIRY

J. M. McCoy Health Center
55555 Pittman Ave.
Columbia, OH 43200

January 1, 2007

Mr. J. Donald
Victor Donald Foundation
44444 Pittman Ave.
Columbia, OH 43200

Dear Mr. Donald:

The founding board of the J. M. McCoy Health Center is writing to inquire about your interest in supporting the work of the J. M. McCoy Health Center, a new facility serving the low income Mill Quarter Neighborhood of Columbia, Ohio. The mission of the health center is to serve the residents of the neighborhood who, because of lack of health insurance, lack of transportation, or lack of trust have had inadequate primary healthcare. The overarching philosophy of the health center is that instilling better health habits, vaccinations, and other preventative care will have greater and longer-lasting benefits to the patient's quality of life. The Victor Donald Foundation has been recommended to us as a supporter of preventative healthcare initiatives.

The founding board is made up of business leaders and healthcare professionals who have witnessed the toll in lost productivity and family disruption from complications of medical conditions left untreated for too long. Lack of access to a primary care provider often results in more expensive emergency room visits, stressing the capacity of the emergency care system as well. In this community, with a large immigrant population, language has also been a barrier to adequate care. The J. M.

SAMPLE LETTER OF INQUIRY

McCoy Health Center will also have multilingual staff on duty at all times. The center will provide counseling and classes for smoking cessation, weight management, and nutrition in its first-year offerings.

The community has responded enthusiastically to the project with volunteers, donations of a facility, pharmaceuticals, and other needs to launch the project. There is an active campaign to create an endowment to cover a portion of future operations costs. If invited to present a full proposal, the health center will request $75,000 to close the gap in first-year operations costs.

We appreciate your consideration of our program and look forward to the opportunity to meet with you to further discuss this request and the work of the health center. For more information please feel free to contact me, Joy Morning, Executive Director, at 614-281-8211. Thank you for your consideration.

Sincerely,

Joy Morning, RN
Executive Director

SAMPLE COVER LETTER

Mr. J. Donald, Grant Review Coordinator
The Victor Donald Foundation
44444 Pittman Avenue
Columbia, OH 43200

January 1, 2007

Applicant:
J. M. McCoy Health Center
55555 Pitman Avenue
Columbia, OH 43200
Telephone: (614) 281-8211
Fax: (614) 222-8889
E-mail: mccoyhealth@internet.org

Dear Mr. J. Donald,

Attached is a request for funding from the J. M. McCoy Health Center, a newly organized community health center. The staff and volunteers of the health center have raised a significant amount of community support for its healthcare service to the low income community known as the Mill Quarter Neighborhood in Columbia, Ohio. The center still faces a shortage of $75,000 for its first-year budget. Because of the Victor Donald Foundation's interest in improving the health status of low income neighborhoods, the J. M. McCoy Health Center hopes that the Foundation will provide a grant for the needed funds.

The center is ready to address any additional questions you may have. You may reach the Grant Contact, Joy Morning, or the Executive Director, Elizabeth Noon, at the above numbers, address, and e-mail.

Thank you for your consideration.

Sincerely,

Joy Morning, Assistant Director
and Grant Contact

SAMPLE GRANT REQUEST

Grant Request from the Victor Donald Foundation
By the J. M. McCoy Health Center

Synopsis:

Grant Contact: Joy Morning
Executive Director: Elizabeth Noon
Staff:

- 2 part-time paid registered nurses (the Executive Director and Assistant Director)
- 25 volunteers
- 5-person board of directors

Tax Status:
The J. M. McCoy Health Center is tax exempt per IRS Section 501(c)(3).

Request for Funding:
$ 75,000 (though any support will be appreciated)

Type of Organization:
Healthcare

Service Area:
Mill Quarter Neighborhood and Mill County

Target Population Served:
Residents of service area needing healthcare

Mission:
To provide free healthcare to members of our community that cannot afford primary care, using an ethnically diverse outreach and advocacy program.

Abstract:
There is great need for primary healthcare in low income neighborhoods in Columbia, Ohio, particularly the Mill Quarter neighborhood, which is ethnically diverse and fast becoming a port of entry for new immigrants to the city.

In general, low income persons and families tend to be uninsured and under-served by the medical community. Recent immigrants tend to be reluctant to approach traditional providers due to language and transportation barriers. Some of the Hispanic community may be reluctant to seek care until an emergency arises, due to concerns about challenges to their legal status.

SAMPLE GRANT REQUEST

Low income populations are far more likely to be affected by controllable conditions such as HIV/AIDS, STDs, obesity, diabetes, high blood pressure, and high cholesterol. Low cost healthcare that is located in the community is essential to reducing the long-term effects of these conditions. Additional services to reach out and educate the residents of the neighborhood about good health habits and the availability of primary care will distinguish this facility. Currently available facilities are unable to adequately serve this growing population.

The J. M. McCoy Health Center will be a new facility in the city and the first of its type in this neighborhood. The executive director and board members all have extensive experience in healthcare, administration, and in serving culturally diverse populations.

Several members of the community have joined the effort to create this facility, including existing healthcare organizations, the local business community, local colleges, technical schools, and community churches. The additional financial support of the Victor Donald Foundation will help make this facility a reality.

Table of Contents:

1. Needs Statement

There is a growing low income population of uninsured individuals and families in Columbia, Ohio, and throughout the nation. The three other neighborhood health centers in the city are overtaxed. They increasingly find it difficult to adequately serve recent immigrants due to cultural and language barriers. The Mill Quarter neighborhood is the only quadrant of the city that does not have a community-based healthcare center. There are no doctors' offices or non-subsidized healthcare facilities in a three-mile radius of the proposed location of the J. M. McCoy Health Center. There is limited access to public transit in this neighborhood, and many of the residents are elderly or have limited mobility. This further limits their access to proactive, primary care health services.

SAMPLE GRANT REQUEST

Columbia is in a growing region of Ohio. The city is home to government offices and several colleges, universities, and technical schools, including the College of Medicine and several schools of nursing. The city hosts a professional hockey team, the Blues, a minor league baseball franchise, and numerous theater, musical, dance, and arts organizations. It is regarded as a community that is economically well diversified and buffered from extreme fluctuations of the state and regional economy.

Nonetheless, almost two-thirds of the residents of this neighborhood have annual incomes of less than 80 percent of the area median of $54,000. One-fourth of the neighborhood arrived in this country in the last five years and are still establishing their families and employment. An estimated 15 percent of the population is over age 65, and approximately one-third of these rely on Social Security and Medicare. The remainder of the low income residents are working in low wage, low skill positions that are often part-time, intermittent, or otherwise do not provide health insurance plans. An estimated 40 percent of this neighborhood does not have access to health insurance. This creates a tremendous need for free primary care throughout the neighborhood.

The three other neighborhood health centers report steady increases in visits and can no longer schedule appointments in less than one week. Even with limited transportation, residents of the Mill Quarter neighborhood accounted for 7.5 percent of neighborhood health center clientele, an increase from 2.5 percent in 2003.

Low income populations and those with inadequate health coverage are more likely to have complications from manageable health conditions such as obesity, high blood pressure, high cholesterol, and sexually transmitted diseases. Simple primary care interventions and education from trusted healthcare providers can significantly reduce the complications of these and other conditions.

Legal and illegal immigration from several countries creates language barriers in providing care, health education, and advocacy to those who need it.

2. Program Description

The health services provided will be extended to all members of the Mill Quarter neighborhood in Columbia, Ohio without consideration of age, race, national origin, religion, family status, or ability to pay. Our outreach and marketing activities will rely heavily on free public announcements in the "What's Going On?" section of the neighborhood newspaper that is delivered free on Thursdays. The five local churches have agreed to place posters on their bulletin boards. The clergy have been involved in planning the program and are committed to referring individuals in

SAMPLE GRANT REQUEST

need of the services to the health center. Also, the local welfare office and United. Appeal are partnering to provide funding and information about the available service to their clients. Joe's Sign Shop is donating a lighted, attractive sign for the front of the building that will make it easy to find the facility.

Volunteers have been recruited from throughout the community, but especially from the medical and nursing schools, local health professionals, and other members of the business community. So far there is a core group of 25 to establish the services and to assist in continuing recruitment of new and replacement volunteers. Particularly sought after will be volunteers who are multilingual in the several languages used in the neighborhood. Eventually it is hoped that some of those who have been served by the health center will be inspired to "give back" by volunteering themselves, both within the center and by reaching out to their neighbors and friends to encourage good health and nutrition habits.

In-kind donations to date have included the sign mentioned above and new and used office equipment and supplies. The building space is being donated by a local property owner, and church groups are assisting with cleanup and painting. Local contractors are volunteering their time to plan and supervise needed renovations to the electrical and plumbing systems. The United Appeal, the County Health Department, and All Saint's Hospital are donating new medical equipment, supplies, medications, and vaccines.

The health center includes a comfortable waiting room outfitted with toys for children, three exam rooms, a private registration booth, a medical records office, secure storage for medications and supplies, separate restrooms for the public and staff, a break area for the volunteers and staff, and a conference/meeting room for training, educational programs, and private consultations.

When individuals visit the health center they will be greeted by a multilingual volunteer who will help determine the reason for the visit and arrange for them to be seen by a nurse immediately if the need appears to be a possible emergency. In the event of a life-threatening emergency, broken bones, and the like, the patient will be sent by EMS to the closest emergency room. The center will have only primary care capabilities, the types of services received at a physician's office: routine physicals, monitoring of chronic conditions, obstetric care, routine lab tests, assistance with smoking cessation, vaccinations, simple suturing, and educational and nutritional counseling. Follow-up care will be scheduled. A case-management approach will be taken, with a medical professional volunteer making contact with the patient to ensure that missed appointments have been rescheduled and medications are

SAMPLE GRANT REQUEST

being taken and being well tolerated. Patients will be linked to partner organizations providing assistance with obtaining long-term needs, such as medical devices or long-term medications.

3. Program Mission, Goals, and Objectives

The mission of the J. M. McCoy Health Center is to improve the lives of the residents of the Mill Quarter neighborhood through better health, healthy habits, and increased connection with the wider community.

The goals for having a community health center in this location are:

a. To make primary healthcare more accessible to those with limited ability to pay, limited transportation, or language barriers

b. To reduce usage of emergency room facilities for non-emergency healthcare

c. To reduce the incidence of serious medical problems that result from progression of unattended medical needs

d. To use health education to improve health habits and reduce the incidence of serious medical problems

Some of these goals are more long-term effects of the immediate activity of delivering primary healthcare and education. But they are the effects that will have long-term major benefits to improve lives of low income families. By helping them remain healthier, they will have fewer missed work or school days. They will have reduced stress if work and income are more stable. Education of the young will be enhanced if attendance is better, which will increase chances for better employment and security in their future. Overall medical costs of treating serious medical conditions will be reduced if simpler interventions are taken before those conditions arise. Medical costs can be reduced over the entire healthcare system if those having little access to primary care are given an affordable alternative to emergency rooms for non-emergency care.

The center plans to start modestly, to use available resources to their maximum benefit, and slowly grow the program as outreach efforts are more successful and demonstrable success attracts more volunteers and funding.

To that end, the first year's measurable objectives include:

SAMPLE GRANT REQUEST

e. To provide primary treatment to 30 patients per day, 5.5 days per week, a total of 8,580 visits per year

f. To provide group health education classes to 10 persons per class, holding two classes per month, for a total of 240 attendees per year. Some individuals may avail themselves of more than one class per year.

g. To achieve an increase of childhood immunizations — such that all neighborhood children will be up to date on their immunization schedule by the end of the year

h. To reduce the number of non-emergency visits by Mill Quarter neighborhood residents to the All Saint's Hospital emergency room by 2,000 per year (from the current 4,000 per year as tracked by zip code of patient)

4. Monitoring and Evaluation

The service will be evaluated and monitored through several mechanisms. Volunteers will assist in the gathering of statistics on usage both daily and compiled. Specific services will be tabulated, such as:

- Children immunized at the center
- Patients screened and/or treated for diabetes and high blood pressure
- Referrals to more advanced care
- Flu shots given
- Number served who do not speak English
- Number assisted in smoking cessation and smoke-free three months later

Along with follow-up care, visitors will be asked to mail back comment cards that may be filled out anonymously regarding their satisfaction with the service and their treatment. There will also be quarterly surveys of the partnering organizations to solicit feedback on their observations of the success of the program based on the experiences of their clientele. The results of surveys and comment cards will be presented in board and staff/volunteer meetings for consideration and discussion as to whether aspects of the service should be adjusted to provide better client confidence and more effective communication and treatment.

SAMPLE GRANT REQUEST

5. Organizational Capacity and Qualifications

The founding board of the J. M. McCoy Health Center formed more than a year ago due to concerns about the healthcare needs of the Mill Quarter neighborhood. The center holds a tax-exempt status under Section 501(c)(3) of the IRS Code. The board of directors now consists of five highly qualified individuals who donate their time to establishing and running the center. Two part-time registered nurses, who also have administrative experience, serve as the centers chief administrator and assistant manager, with at least one providing coverage during all hours of operation. Volunteer medical board certified nurse practitioners and physicians provide the actual medical evaluations, and treatments and prescribe any necessary medications. The full résumés of key individuals are available upon request. These key individuals and their roles are as follows:

Board President	Harriet Smith, MD, Women's Health Center
Board Vice-President	Harold Smose, MD, All Saint's Hospital Psychiatry Department
Board Treasurer	Harry Jones, CPA, Smith & Jones LLC
Board Member	Hazel Thoms, Ph.D., Professor of Foreign Languages, All Saint's College
Board Member	Henrietta Toopes, Owner, Best Ever Cookie Company
Chief Administrator	Hubert Underwood, RN, MBA
Assistant Director	Hallie Ulrich, RN

6. Budget and Long-Term Sustainability

The capital improvements to the building are nearly complete, and the center should be able to open in six months. These are being donated to the center as in-kind donations. The budget therefore reflects nearly all operational costs. Only a few pieces of equipment remain to be purchased and will be purchased through a separate capital campaign.

SAMPLE GRANT REQUEST

ITEM	COST PER UNIT	EXTENDED COST FOR YEAR
Salaries and Fringes	$60,000 ea	$120,000
Utilities/Telephone/Internet	$1,000/month	$12,000
Office Supplies	$500/month	$6,000
Medical Supplies, donated	$1,000/month	$0
Medical Supplies, purchased	$2,000/month	$24,000
Volunteer Recognition Program	$100 ea	$250
Insurance, property	$1,000	$1,000
Cleaning and Maintenance	$250/month	$3,000
Total Year		$166,250

Revenues to the center will be limited, as most of the expected patients will not have access to health insurance. Medical education classes charge a nominal $5 per class fee, and one partner organization, Mill Quarter Veterans of America, has pledged to provide ten scholarships each month to those who cannot afford this amount. Total income expected: $1,200 per year. Other pledges for this year include:

- The United Appeal has pledged: $50,000
- The Central Ohio Community Foundation has pledged: $45,000

The Donor Relations Committee, a special committee of five volunteers that is headed up by one of the board members, is responsible for special fund-raising to create an endowment to cover some of the long-term overhead and maintenance expenses of the center. Currently this includes direct appeals to community members and donation boxes that will be distributed to supportive businesses in the community, as well as in the center itself. Though patients will not be charged for services, they will have the opportunity to contribute something anonymously at the donation boxes. Other large fund-raisers will be planned, as well as solicitation of legacy gifts (contributions directly from the estates of deceased supporters), as the committee becomes more organized. The plan is to raise $500,000 per year for the next six years, and with cautious investment management, this should generate enough investment income to fund operations at current levels after that time.

The center does not expect to become totally financially independent. There will always be a need for some support from the community and special opportunity grants. The Donor Relations Committee, as well as the board of directors and the executive director, will have responsibility for maintaining relationships with

SAMPLE GRANT REQUEST

community stakeholders and community connection to and awareness of the beneficial work of the center.

7. Summary

The J. M. McCoy Health Center fills a substantial gap in the delivery of primary healthcare in the low income Mill Quarter neighborhood. With its emphasis on outreach and advocacy with a multilingual capacity, it will gain the trust of those in the community that have been reluctant to seek out healthcare. The primary healthcare approach will focus on preventative care through vaccinations, counseling, and classes that promote better health and nutrition habits. In the long term the center will enhance the overall quality of life for the neighborhood residents through better health and affordable care. Area hospitals will have less pressure on their emergency services as individuals seek out primary care at the appropriate level and before deferred issues become medical emergencies.

The health center is already receiving significant community support and should be able to generate some of its own funds in the future in addition to donations and grants.

The J. M. McCoy Health Center is an excellent match with the interests of the Victor Donald Foundation. The staff and leadership have worked hard to bring the project this far and look forward to being able to start operations with all their planned programming in place with a grant from the Foundation. The Foundation's consideration is greatly appreciated.

8. Appendices

Copies of Letters of Commitment and Support

Copies of News Articles and Press Releases

PROPOSAL TEMPLATE

Fill in the blanks or answer the question and delete the prompts. Fill in more detailed information as needed. Revise as needed per individual foundation requirements.

COVER LETTER
(From) Letter Head (or your name and address) Date:________________________________ (To) Contact Name:__________________________ Foundation Name:__________________________ Foundation Address:________________________ City, State, Zip Code:______________________ Dear M_(title)__(name)________: The (name of organization) is pleased to submit this proposal for grant funding under the (name of grant program/category). The (name of organization)'s (name of project or program) has been created to solve the problem of (state the major need) by (state the major activities). The (name of project or program) addresses the concerns of the (name of foundation/ and category or grant program name) because (state the features of the program that relate to the stated mission or interests of the funder). The (name of organization) has obtained monetary and/or in-kind support from the following: (list organizations, companies, and community leaders that have already pledged support). The amount of this request: ($XX,XXX). For further information, please contact: (Primary contact name, title, phone number, and address) at (any other facts, such as office hours). Sincerely, (Signature of writer or CEO) (Typed Name and Title)

TABLE OF CONTENTS	
Cover Letter	Pg
Abstract	Pg
Table of Contents	Pg
Needs Statement	Pg
Program Description	Pg
Monitoring and Evaluation	Pg
Goals and Measurable Objectives	Pg
Budget	Pg
Appendices	Pg

ABSTRACT OF PROPOSAL

Request From: (Name of Applicant)________________

Total Project Cost: ____________________

Contact Name:__________________________________

Other Funds Committed:________________

Mailing Address:_______________________________

Amount of This Request:________________

Name of Project:_______________________________

Address of Project:_____________________________ (May be different than the organization's main office)

Target Clientele: ____

____

Project Synopsis: (Briefly state why this project is needed): ____________________

____

____

(Briefly state the activity): ____

____

____

(Briefly state the method of delivery): _____________________________________

____

____

(Briefly state the benefits to be attained by sponsoring this project): ____________

____

____

(Briefly state the number of units of service to be delivered): ________________

____

____

DESCRIPTION OF ORGANIZATION

1. When was the organization founded: ______

2. Mission of the applicant: ______

3. What role does it fulfill in the community: ______

4. State the connection between the funder's objectives and the activities of this applicant: ______

5. Names of board members: ______

6. Skills they possess: ______

7. Résumés of staff members: ______

8. The applicant's accomplishments: ______

9. How many staff and volunteers are there: ______

STATEMENT OF NEED

1. This program was designed to address the problem of: ______________________

2. The number of people affected by this problem: ______________________

3. Special characteristics of those affected: ______________________

4. Barriers to resolution of the problem: ______________________

5. Source of this information: ______________________

6. Other efforts that address the problem: ______________________

7. Gap between size of problem and available resources: ______________________

8. Cite other studies of the problem: ______________________

9. Attach tables and graphs to illustrate the magnitude of the problem: ______________________

PROGRAM DESCRIPTION

1. Who: ______________________________

2. Does What: ______________________________

3. When: ______________________________

4. Where: ______________________________

5. Why: ______________________________

6. How: ______________________________

7. Tell how the community has supported the organization and/or this project: ______________________________

8. Is this project duplicated in the community: ______________________________

9. Can this project be replicated easily in other communities: ______________________________

10. What is the project budget — revenues and expenses: ______________________________

PROGRAM DESCRIPTION

11. What is the long-term financial plan for the organization and program: ________

    a. Other funding sources: ________

    b. In-kind donation of services and materials: ________

GOALS AND OBJECTIVES

1. What is the unit of service: ________

2. How many units will be delivered: ________

3. Secondary impacts: ________

4. How many of those: ________

PROGRAM EVALUATION

1. Who will be responsible for program oversight: ______________________

2. How will evaluations be conducted: ______________________

3. How often will the program be evaluated: ______________________

4. Who will review the evaluations: ______________________

5. What will be the involvement of the board: ______________________

6. What financial controls will be used: ______________________

7. Address specific evaluation requirements of the funder: ______________________

SUMMARY

1. Closing statement summarizing the importance of this project in the community:

___

2. Restate the connection between the funder's objectives and the purpose of this project: ___

3. Reminder that the funder's support is vital to accomplishing the mission:

___

4. Thank them for their consideration and support: ___

APPENDICES

1. Copies of relevant media articles: ______

2. Letters of support: ______

3. Other exhibits that illustrate data: ______

4. Certifications required by funder: ______

5. Résumés, if needed: ______

6. Copies of audit reports, if required: ______

7. Copies of IRS letter of determination of tax exempt status, if required: ______

8. Portfolio material, if requested: ______

9. Photographs, videos, and the like, only if permitted: ______

SAMPLE GOVERNMENT GRANT

Section A: Project Synopsis

Grant Title: MICROBUSINESS GRANT PROGRAM

Applicant Information: ______________________________

Grant Submission Date: ______________________________

Name of Community: ______________________________

Contact Person and Title: ______________________________

Address: ______________________________

Phone: ______________________________

Fax: ______________________________

E-mail: ______________________________

Resolution to make application date of passage: ______________________________

Resolution number: ______________________________

Federal Tax ID #: ______________________________

Project Budget: ______________________________

Matching Funds: ______________________________

Value In-kind Services: ______________________________

SAMPLE GOVERNMENT GRANT

Grant Request:__________________________________

Program Goals:__________________________________

Section B: Need Statement

Though the city has enjoyed gains in its economy, its status continues to lag behind other communities in the county with respect to some economic measures. The median household income in 1999 was still only $35,681. The unemployment rate for the city tends to be similar to the county as a whole, which in June of 2005 was 5.7 percent, up from less than 5 percent in 2004. During the city's annual planning process, micro-business development was adopted as a strategy to assist low income households with creating their own job opportunities and self-reliance. The city first attempted a microbusiness program in 1992. The community was unable to loan out all the funds available, and a few loans have defaulted over the years. However, a few loans were successful and have generated enough program income to make two more loans since the end of the program.

The city gained valuable experience from this effort and has made design changes for the current proposal. The ability to use program income has maintained interest and knowledge of the program in the intervening years.

The JVS Business Enterprise Center (BEC) now offers the training and technical assistance on an individualized basis, rather than on a fixed college calendar. This removes the barrier of time and scheduling that was an issue in the 1992 program.

The previous experience indicated that loan recipients needed a more structured follow-up program to keep them accountable to their plans and to provide interventions during the difficult first year. This should prevent loan delinquencies and defaults. The city learned that it is important to keep the door open for restructuring of loans to help applicants get past difficult business periods. This year's program design features incentives, like free additional training in small business management, as a reward for completing three hours of counseling with the business coach (from the BEC) and the opportunity to "pass a payment" for each set of 11 on-time payments over the course of the loan to help with difficult cash flow periods.

Section C: Program Description

Because the city is the grantee for these funds, the program will be limited to residents of the city that are seeking to operate businesses within the city. The program will be available city wide.

SAMPLE GOVERNMENT GRANT

This program aims to increase employment opportunities for persons unemployed or under-employed in the current marketplace or for those with an entrepreneurial spirit through the creation or expansion of microbusinesses. Small businesses have produced 71 percent of the 1.9 million new jobs created nationally between 1993 and 1997 and employ 54 percent of the private work force. These small enterprises are often considered too high risk for traditional lenders, and in a recent survey, 64 percent of one-year-old firms indicated that obtaining capital is their biggest concern.

Within the population, there are a number of households that tend to be less likely to participate in the traditional employment market and are less likely to access financing for small businesses through traditional lenders. These include those on ADC, unemployed, part-time employed, homemakers re-entering the work force, or any low income person interested in starting his or her own business. In particular, 17.5 percent of the city's households are of very low income (less than 50 percent of AMGI) and 56.7 percent of these are single parent households, all of whom, due to life situations or prejudice, may have difficulty obtaining employment in the general labor market. Home-based businesses provide a popular option for parents of small children at all income ranges.

The city is in the process of creating a set of marketing materials to be distributed to low to moderate-income households to encourage their participation. These will include brochures, posters, and flyers to be distributed in as many locations as possible. These will include grocery stores, the Salvation Army offices, the homeless center, and the college extension office. There will be frequent newspaper press releases, as well as promotions on the public access television station, the city's Web site, and the city's newsletter.

Marketing of the program will be aimed at encouraging participation from the demographic groups cited above. Information concerning the program will be distributed through the city's partners in community development efforts, including those represented in the loan review committee, as well as the YWCA and YMCA, the Public Library, and the city's Community Development Office.

All partners sitting on the loan review committee will promote the program at their office locations, in public appearances they make to community groups, as well as in their general membership/staff meetings. The Business Enterprise Center will promote information about the availability of tuition grants to their students and in recruiting materials.

SAMPLE GOVERNMENT GRANT

Eligibility for the Program

Applicants:

- The business must employ five or fewer employees, including the owner.
- The business must be operating legally with proper licensing and not be delinquent in county, state, federal taxes, unemployment insurance, or workers' compensation premiums.
- The business must not be in arrears in payroll or more than 60 days in arrears on any obligations to suppliers, utilities, rent, and so forth.
- The successful applicant must complete the Small Business Enterprise Center's Microbusiness Training Program prior to receiving loan funds. Tuition cost for this program will be provided by the City Microbusiness Program as a grant.
- Upon completion of the training program and prior to use of loan funds, the applicant must have completed market research, a business plan, and set up an accounting system.
- Recipients of loan funds will be encouraged to participate in follow-up counseling and complete the Small Business Management series of training.
- The BEC will provide additional follow-up counseling monthly for one year after business startup, at no additional cost.

Eligible Uses of Loans

- The City Microbusiness Grant Program funds may be used as follows:
    - To purchase capital equipment
    - For working capital (merchandise stock and supplies)
    - To make improvements in store interiors
    - To purchase store fixtures (for displays and the like)
- Ineligible Uses — The funds may not be used to pay salaries, fringe benefits, rent, or utilities

SAMPLE GOVERNMENT GRANT

Section D: Goals

1) Tuition for training and technical assistance will provide ten applicants with Microbusiness Development Training at an average cost of $700 each.

2) Five recipients of direct loans or working capital loans will be given additional tuition grants of $600 for extended BEC counseling.

3) The program intends to provide loans to five microbusinesses at an average of $8,900 each, with a maximum loan available of up to $10,000. It is expected that some, but not all, applicants will need both direct loans and working capital loans.

4) To strengthen a collaborative program with local agencies to stimulate microbusiness and to provide ongoing mentoring/coaching relationships with graduates with individualized follow-up counseling specific to their own businesses and situations.

5) To deliver further individualized training that goes into greater depth than the initial " curriculum" at a point when the business is ready for more sophisticated tools.

6) To provide the entrepreneur with a pathway to develop a relationship with a local lender for financial services and future capital needed to sustain the business successfully in the long-term future.

7) To continue the program in future years, built by a revolving loan pool from loan repayments.

Outcome	Measurement	Average Cost	Total Cost	(Maximum)
Microbusiness Training	10	$700	$7,000	$70 per hour
Small Business Management Training (advanced counseling)	5	$600	$3,000	$70 per hour
Business Loans (Combined direct loans and/or working capital)	5	$8,900	$44,500	$10,000

SAMPLE GOVERNMENT GRANT

Recruitment of interested individuals is already in process, and assistance will be provided on a first-come/first-served basis if the city's grant application is funded. Recruitment will continue until all available loan funds are committed. This is a 12-month program starting in approximately December.

Monitoring Payments and Project Process

- The loan review committee (LRC) will receive monthly reports of each applicant's attendance and progress in the training courses and upon the completion of the business plan.
- Upon final loan approval by the LRC, the applicant will be notified and a loan closing will be scheduled at the city Community Development Department.
- A purchase order for the loan amount will be processed. To the extent feasible, checks will be issued.

In the event of numerous small purchases, the applicant will be required to submit invoices or proof of delivery/payment of the items. The CD director will later visit the premises and attempt to verify that appropriate purchases have been made and make a note in the file.

- The city will provide the applicant with payment coupons to be used with each month's payment. Payments will be sent directly to the city auditor's office, payable to the Microbusiness Account. The Finance Department will levy a $10 per month processing fee on each loan.
- The city auditor will transfer payments to the lender partner in proportion to their participation in each loan on agreed-upon intervals, with a statement of loan status and receivables for the covered period.
- The auditor's office will provide to the LRC monthly reports of payments and fund balances. Reminder notices will be sent if payments become more than 15 days late and again if 30 days late.
- If payments are 30 days late, the Training and Technical Assistance Provider will be requested to make contact with the business owner to provide intervention and counseling services. Renegotiation of the loan will be permitted if recommended to the LRC by the counselor.

SAMPLE GOVERNMENT GRANT

- If payments become more than 90 days late without attempts to negotiate a solution, collection proceedings will begin.
- Recipients who successfully complete eleven (11) months in good standing will be allowed to "pass a payment" during any selected month thereafter, with the interest being added on to the end of the loan.

Recipients who successfully complete the course and remain in good standing regarding loan payments will be able to use the city's program as a positive credit reference in future credit requests.

Section E: Organization Description and Qualifications

The city Microbusiness Grant Program will be administered by the City Community Development (CD) Office with the assistance of a local review committee. The City CD Office in 1992 administered a Microbusiness Grant Program, which still provides a small amount of program income.

All training and technical assistance will be provided through a partnership with the JVS Business Enterprise Center (BEC). The BEC is an outstanding resource for the city's microbusiness training needs. It already operates a microbusiness program serving low income residents in the unincorporated areas of a four-county area, which includes W, X, Y, and Z Counties. The program was established to serve new and growing companies. Their mission statement is:

"The JVS Business Enterprise Center is dedicated to community economic development and to serve as a resource for business startups and expansions."

Organization of the Microbusiness Grant Program

The program will be a collaborative with representatives that make up the loan review committee (LRC).

These are:

- The City Community Development Director
- JVS Business Enterprise Center Instructor
- Local Lender Partner/ Local Bank's Representative

SAMPLE GOVERNMENT GRANT

The City's Community Development Director will have ultimate responsibility for functions of administration, as well as serving as the loan review committee liaison representing the city's interests as grant recipients. The JVS Business Enterprise Center will be providing the training and technical assistance component of the program. Its experience and insight in this area will strengthen the assessments of an applicant's potential to succeed with this assistance. The local lender partner, Local Bank, will serve on the loan review committee to represent the lender's interests in underwriting a portion of each loan. Its representative will have responsibility for cultivating a business relationship with the applicant, linking it to other financial services, such as business checking accounts, and supporting it in developing a capacity to access future capital for expansion as needed. Direct program administration will primarily involve those described briefly above.

The CD Director will have responsibility for document preparation, scheduling, filing, and telephone contacts. Résumés are included at the end of this section.

Section F: Budget Summary Table

Activity Name	Total Cost	CDBG Federal	Other Funds	Outcomes
Direct Loans	$26,700	$21,000	$5,700	3 loans
Working Capital Loans	$17,800	$14,000	$3,800	2 loans
Subtotal	$44,500	$35,000	$9,500	5 loans
Training/Technical Assistance	$10,000	$10,000		10 training 5 tech assistance
Administration	$5,000	$5,000		1 program year
Total	$59,500	$50,000	$9,500	

Section G: Program Sustainability

This program will be sustainable over a great time period as loan repayments revolve to new loans. The city will attempt to recruit new applicants from students already enrolled in the JVS Entrepreneurial program in order to minimize expenditures for the training component and to maximize the available funds for overcoming other costs of business startup and expansion. The number of new

SAMPLE GOVERNMENT GRANT

loans funded will stabilize to one to two per year. The City CD Department can absorb the monitoring activities for this level of activity within its current staffing and resources.

Federal SF 424

Common Grant Application Forms

APPLICATION FOR FEDERAL ASSISTANCE (SF 424)

2. DATE SUBMITTED

Application Identifier

1. TYPE OF SUBMISSION
Application
☐ Construction
☐ Non-Construction
Pre-Application
☐ Construction
☐ Non-Construction

3. DATE RECEIVED BY STATE

State Application Identifier

4. DATE RECEIVED BY FEDERAL AGENCY

Federal Identifier

Legal Name

Organizational Unit

Address *(city, county, state, and zip code):*

Name and telephone number of the person to be contacted on matters involving this application *(give area code):*

6. EMPLOYER IDENTIFICATION NUMBER (EIN):
☐☐–☐☐☐☐☐☐☐

7. TYPE OF APPLICANT (*enter appropriate letter in box)*

A. State
B. County
C. Municipal
D. Township
E. Interstate
F. Intermunicipal
G. Special District
H. Independent School District
I. State Controlled Institution of Higher Learning
J. Private University
K. Indian Tribe
L. Individual
M. Profit Organization
N. Other (Specify) ______

8. TYPE OF APPLICATION
☐ New ☐ Continuation ☐ Revision
If Revision, enter appropriate letter(s) in box(es): ☐ ☐
A. Increase Award B. Decrease Award C. Increase Duration
D. Decrease Duration Other *(specify)*
______

9. NAME OF FEDERAL AGENCY:

10. CATALOG FEDERAL DOMESTIC ASSISTANCE NUMBER: ☐☐.☐☐☐

TITLE:

11. DESCRIPTIVE TITLE OF APPLICANT'S PROJECT:

12. AREAS AFFECTED BY PROJECT *(cities, counties, states, etc.):*

13. PROPOSED PROJECT:

Start Date	End Date

14. CONGRESSIONAL DISTRICT OF:
a. Applicant
b. Project

15. ESTIMATED FUNDING:

a.	Federal	$	.00
b.	Applicant	$	.00
c.	State	$	.00
d.	Local	$	.00
e.	Other	$	.00
f.	Program Income	$	.00
g.	TOTAL	$	.00

16. IS APPLICATION SUBJECT TO REVIEW BY STATE EXECUTIVE ORDER 12372 PROCESS?

a. YES THIS PREAPPLICATION/APPLICATION WAS MADE AVAILABLE TO THE STATE EXECUTIVE ORDER 12372 PROCESS FOR REVIEW ON

DATE_

b. NO ☐ PROGRAM IS NOT COVERED BY E.O. 12372

☐ OR PROGRAM HAS NOT BEEN SELECTED BY STATE FOR REVIEW

17. IS THE APPLICANT DELINQUENT ON ANY FEDERAL DEBT?

☐ Yes If "Yes" attach an explanation ☐ No

18. TO THE BEST OF MY KNOWLEDGE AND BELIEF ALL DATA IN THIS APPLICATION AND PREAPPLICATION ARE TRUE AND CORRECT. THE DOCUMENT HAS BEEN DULY AUTHORIZED BY THE GOVERNING BODY OF THE APPLICANT AND THE APPLICANT WILL COMPLY WITH THE ATTACHED ASSURANCES IF THE ASSISTANCE IS AWARDED.

a. Typed Name of Authorized Representative	b. Title	c. Telephone number
d. Signature of Authorized Representative		e. Date Signed

SAMPLES OF OTHER HELPFUL TOOLS

- Grant Sources Evaluation Tool
- Grant Writing Schedule and Checklist

Grant Sources Evaluation Tool — Sample

Scenario: Community Group A wants to renovate a historic building to use for a museum and offices. It is looking for rare funds to pay for the renovation work. Since nonprofits do not pay taxes, to use the tax credits it must go through a complicated process called syndication, in which it will "sell" the credits to a for-profit partner for a slightly lesser amount of cash.

Name of Grant Program	Name of Foundation	Eligible Entities	Funding Priorities	Date Due	Amount Available	We Apply? Yes or No
Challenge Grant	Kresge Foundation	Nonprofits & Govts.	* Build local $ support * Allows capital projects ** LEED compliance	March 15	$300,000	Yes
Historic Properties Credit	State Historic Preservation Office	Any	*Renovation work compliant with historic standards	April 15	10% of costs up to $50,000 (tax credit that will have to be syndicated)	Yes
Community Preservation Fund	Local Community Foundation	Nonprofits	*Community groups, non-capital expenses	Feb 15	$ 1,000	No

Name of Grant Program	Name of Foundation	Eligible Entities	Funding Priorities	Date Due	Amount Available	We Apply? Yes or No
Total Possible					$350,000	
Total Match Required					$500,000 ($500,000 to achieve maximum credit will also meet the $300,000 match for Kresge)	
Total Budget					$850,000	

**LEED compliance = Leadership in Energy Efficiency and Design, by the Green Building Council

In this example, the applicant might simply choose to apply for less than the maximum tax credit or less than the maximum of the Challenge Grant if matching requirements are unattainable by the grant period or if not required by the budget.

SAMPLE GRANT WRITING SCHEDULE/CHECKLIST

Note: *Shorten as necessary according to available time until due date.*

		Week 1	Week 2	Week 3	Week 4	Week 5	Week 6	Due Date	Announcement Date
Identify need	x								
Develop concept	x								
Research and select grants	x								
Obtain guidelines	x								
Letter of inquiry or intent	x								
Pre-submission conference		x							
Write project summary (abstract)		x							
Write needs statement			x						
Write program description			x						
Write goals and measurable objectives				x					
Write evaluation plan				x					
Obtain cost estimates					x				

		Week 1	Week 2	Week 3	Week 4	Week 5	Week 6	Due Date	Announcement Date
Develop budget					x				
Write description of organization						x			
Write future sustainability						x			
Format & edit							x		
Write & attach cover letter							x		
Printing, binding, shipping							x		
Due date								x	
Announce-ment date									x

AUTHOR DEDICATION & BIOGRAPHY

I am forever indebted to Marsha, my first editor, Bruce, Ken, Jean, Al, and many others for their contributions, friendship, and insights. I am grateful to the many funders I have worked with over the years for their guidance, awards, and encouragement. Thanks to my family for their belief in me, for their patience and understanding, which made the long hours bearable. Certainly, and not least, were it not for Angela's gentle prodding and the immeasurable help of the editors at Atlantic Publishing, this book would not have been possible.

Dianne Harris has spent years in volunteer service and fundraising of all types for her many favorite causes. She feels fortunate to have engaged in grant writing and grant administration as a profession. She spent her early career working in the medical field where she grew committed to improving the health and opportunities of the less fortunate. She developed an interest in saving historic buildings and towns after witnessing the craftsmanship of her great aunt's brick Victorian home. As a mother, she grew concerned with issues of education, play, music and the arts as vital parts of human development. Her parents settled her family in rural Ohio near the Lake Erie shore at the same time as thousands came from the south and from around the world to work in the northern factories. She was educated at the urban campus of The Ohio State University, where she came to love city life as much as the countryside and the waterfront. Grant writing and town planning have allowed her to engage her diverse interests, and to develop friendships with those from all walks of life. She still resides, plans, and writes grants in central Ohio with her husband of 22 years, her two almost-grown sons, and her cherished pets.

INDEX

A

B

C

D

E

S

T

V

W